378.17 CHA
ST

P. 92
→ Students feedback

P. 119 → Tourism.

Interdisciplinary Learning

Southampton
SOLENT
University

MOUNTBATTEN LIBRARY
Tel: 023 8031 9249

As
sul
mu
stu
spe
bo

issu
inf

Gr
pra
tea

Bal
op

Ste
Nutrition Science in the University of Chester, England.

Interdisciplinary Learning and Teaching in Higher Education

Theory and Practice

Edited by Balasubramanyam Chandramohan and
Stephen Fallows

Routledge
Taylor & Francis Group

NEW YORK AND LONDON

In memory of my
parents (Thiru Balasubramanyan and Tirumati Nagaveni) and
younger brother (Karthigeyan – also known as Vettri)
Chandramohan

First published 2009
by Routledge
270 Madison Ave, New York, NY 10016

Simultaneously published in the U.K.
by Routledge
2 Park Square, Milton Park, Abingdon, Oxon OX14 4RN

Routledge is an imprint of the Taylor & Francis Group, an informa business

© 2009 Taylor & Francis

Typeset in Minion by
Swales & Willis Ltd, Exeter, Devon
Printed and bound in the United States of America on acid-free paper by
Walsworth Publishing Company, Marceline, MO

Library of Congress Cataloging in Publication Data
Interdisciplinary learning and teaching in higher education : theory and practice / editors, Balasubramanyam Chandramohan and Steve Fallows.
p. cm.
Includes bibliographical references and index.
1. Interdisciplinary approach in education.   2. Education, Higher—Curricula.   I. Chandramohan, Balasubramanyam, 1955–   II. Fallows, Stephen J.
LB2361.I488 2008
378.1'25—dc22   2007041771

ISBN10: 0–415–34131–0 (hbk)
ISBN10: 0–415–34130–2 (pbk)
ISBN10: 0–203–92870–9 (ebk)

ISBN13: 978–0–415–34131–8 (hbk)
ISBN13: 978–0–415–34130–1 (pbk)
ISBN13: 978–0–203–92870–7 (ebk)

Contents

Part I
Horizontal: Matters that Apply across Entire Programs

Figures and Tables

Contributors

Dr Balasubramanyam Chandramohan is a Senior Lecturer in Academic Development at Kingston University, England and teaches on the Post-graduate Certificate in Learning and Teaching in Higher Education. He is a member of the Association for Integrative Studies (U.S.) and coedits *Imperium*, an interdisciplinary online journal, www.imperiumjournal.com.
Email: b.chandramohan@kingston.ac.uk

Professor R. J. Ellis is Head of Department of American and Canadian Studies at the University of Birmingham, England. He is the Research Co-ordinator of American and Canadian Studies at the university, Editorial Advisor (Commissioning Editor [American Texts]), Trent Editions, and Editor, Comparative American Studies (CAS).
http://www.uscanada.bham.ac.uk/staff/ellis.html

Dr Stephen Fallows is Deputy Director of the Centre for Exercise and Nutrition Science in the University of Chester, England. His responsibilities relate to research management and quality assurance across three major interdisciplinary post-graduate health-related programs delivered in the U.K., Ireland, Singapore, Hong Kong, and India.
http://www.chester.ac.uk/cens/staff.html

Professor Lee Harvey is Director of Research and Evaluation at the Higher Education Academy, U.K. He was until recently Director of the Centre for Research and Evaluation at Sheffield Hallam University.
http://www.heacademy.ac.uk

Dr Susan Illingworth is a member of the Research Ethics Committee of the University of Leeds, England. She coordinated the ETHICS project, a cross-disciplinary initiative aimed to promote examples of effective practice in ethics learning and teaching, drawing on philosophical and religious studies, bioscience, law, medicine, dentistry and veterinary medicine, psychology, and health sciences and practice.

Ms Kate Irving is Senior Academic Development Adviser at the Learning and Teaching Institute, University of Chester, where she has responsibility for development of CPD opportunities for colleagues working in all areas of academic practice. She is also responsible for the development of pedagogic

research at the university and is a member of the Higher Education Academy's Expert Group on the Pedagogy of Work Force Development.
http://www.chester.ac.uk/cwrs/staff.html

Dr Tazim Jamal is Associate Professor at the Department of Recreation, Parks, and Tourism Sciences in Texas A&M University, U.S. She has instructed on philosophy of social science in relation to tourism studies. Her specialties include: community-based and collaborative tourism planning, heritage tourism, sustainable tourism theory and practice; research on multi-stakeholder collaborations convened to address natural resource sustainability, and tourism-related conflicts.
http://rptsweb.tamu.edu/faculty/Jamal/index.html

Dr Dawn Jourdan is Assistant Professor of Landscape Architecture and Urban Planning at Texas A&M University, U.S. She conducts research pertaining to planning law, historic preservation, and intergenerational participation; teaches planning history and theory, planning law and legislation, real estate law, and historic preservation law. Her research focuses on the reduction of grief effects experienced by those relocated as a result of urban renewal.
http://archone.tamu.edu/laup/People/Faculty/faculty_profile/Jourdan.html

Professor Allison Littlejohn is Chair of Learning Technology at Glasgow Caledonian University, Scotland. She is also the Director of the Caledonian Academy: an academic support centre integrating research, advanced scholarship, and transformational change in learning innovation. Allison leads a range of research projects exploring learning innovation and educational development, learning design, learning technology interoperability, and professional development in higher education.
http://www.academy.gcal.ac.uk/people/littlejohn.html

Dr Susana Lorenzo-Zamorano is a Teaching Fellow in Spanish Studies at the University of Manchester, England. She teaches "Interdisciplinarity in the Undergraduate Curriculum", a funded project that evaluates the feasibility of interdisciplinary learning with undergraduates. During 2004–2005 she took part in an interdisciplinary project at the university involving Spanish, geography, education, medicine, and biological sciences.
http://www.llc.manchester.ac.uk/aboutus/staff/splas/SLorenzo/

Dr Justin Meggitt is a Fellow, and Senior Lecturer in the Study of Religion and the Origins of Christianity at the University of Cambridge, England. He is also a member of The Jesus Project, an international initiative of The Committee for the Scientific Examination of Religion (CSER), and one of

those responsible for the university's new Master of Studies in the Study of Jewish-Christian Relations.
http://www.christianorigins.org/

Dr David Nicol is Reader and Deputy Director of the Centre for Academic Practice and Learning Enhancement (CAPLE), University of Strathclyde in Glasgow, Scotland. He is the primary named contact in the Centre for the Faculty of Engineering. He also directs Re-Engineering Assessment Practices in Scottish Higher Education (REAP), a project led by the Centre.
http://www.strath.ac.uk/caple/staff/nicoldaviddr

Robert J. Petrausch EdD is Assistant Professor of Mass Communication at Iona College, New Rochelle, NY. He has a broad background in media relations, speech writing, program planning, public relations management, and training and teaches in the public relations sequence at the undergraduate and graduate level. His research interests include public relations, public speaking, organizational communications, and organizational learning in both profit and non-profit organizations.
http://www.iona.edu/academic/artsscience/departments/masscomm/faculty/bpetrausch.cfm

Professor Derek Raine teaches at the Department of Physics at the University of Leicester, England. Commenting on his work he says: "In leading the planning of curricula in Physics and in our new Interdisciplinary Sciences program I also need to keep up with developments in research into the teaching of physics ... the programs take account of advances in our understanding of how students learn."
http://www.le.ac.uk/admissions/ugprospectus/profiles_derek.html

Professor Lorraine Stefani is Director of the Centre for Academic Development at the University of Auckland, New Zealand. The Centre's work focuses on professional development of staff, student learning, and flexible and distance learning. Her current research interests and projects include: scholarship of teaching and learning, e-Portfolios for students, the impact of academic development on student learning outcomes, and assessment of student learning.
http://cad.auckland.ac.nz/index.php?p=staff_detail.php&upi=lste066

Professor A. Sundaram is Professor and Head of the Department of Futures Studies in the School of Energy, Environment and Natural Resources at Madurai Kamaraj University, Madurai, Tamil Nadu State, India. He teaches and supervises research in Geographical Information System (GIS).
http://www.mkuniversity.org/SC_ENERGY.HTM

Ms Gwen van der Velden is Director of Learning and Teaching Enhancement at the University of Bath, England. Gwen leads a team that is responsible for educational development, the quality management of learning and teaching, academic staff development related to learning and teaching, and e-learning support and development.
http://www.bath.ac.uk/learningandteaching/?page_id=293

Dr Shân Wareing is Dean of Learning and Teaching Development at the University of the Arts, London, where she has responsibility for developing and implementing the Learning and Teaching Strategy, the eLearning Strategy, and building a culture of pedagogic research. Her interests include educational development practice and students' study skills. She is Co-Chair of the U.K. based Staff and Educational Development Association (SEDA).
http://www.arts.ac.uk/itrdu/people/people_shan_2.htm

Dr Melanie Wright is Fellow, Tutor and Director of Studies in Theology and Religious Studies, Girton College, Cambridge University. She is Course Director for the Master of Studies in the Study of Jewish-Christian Relations and paper coordinator for the "Culture" paper. In addition, she lectured in Modern Judaism and Religion and Film for Cambridge University (Divinity Faculty and Institute of Continuing Education) in 2006–2007.
http://www.cjcr.cam.ac.uk/staff/wright.html

Foreword

We live in interdisciplinary times. Whereas historically students frequently chose courses to study at university based on their love of a particular subject at school, with little thought for what this might lead to on graduation, nowadays students are more likely to select their programmes with a career in mind and these often cross disciplines. Students studying drama or health studies, for example, are likely to encounter elements of marketing and finance within their courses, leading to capability in arts management or health promotion. Even students studying subjects like fine art or creative writing are likely to find required elements in their courses that include enterprise education, representing a realistic approach to employability, since graduates in these disciplines are likely to self-manage patchwork careers that will require them to demonstrate an entrepreneurial approach to self-promotion.

Web 2.0-aware students, used to locating and using content from multiple (frequently web-based) sources and to sharing ideas through diverse social and other networks, often find our divisions of learning content into separate silos arbitrary, unhelpful, and mystifying. Creative curriculum designers and managers take this logic into account and develop eclectic and flexible learning programmes that can accommodate students' needs better than traditional approaches ever could.

Similarly, fewer students enter higher education nowadays straight from school, and so they bring with them life-experiences and competences that educators ignore at their peril. Even notionally full-time students today in many countries hold down part-time jobs alongside their studies, so work-related learning that helps them integrate personal and professional development into their programmes of study can enrich and deepen their learning experiences.

Pedagogically, many are convinced that the best way to encourage students to be active learners is to get them to apply themselves to problems that cross subject boundaries and encourage creative thinking, unbounded by subject constraints. Such approaches need integrated academic development so that staff are supported to be innovative in curriculum delivery, assessment, and evaluation.

I welcome this publication, exploring as it does how we can best design, organise, implement, and review interdisciplinary learning and teaching in higher education. Readers will no doubt value both the whole-programme approaches described here and the useful illustrative examples contained in the second half of the book, which both illustrate and theorise interdisciplinarity in practice. With a very distinguished set of international contributors who generously share their experience-enriched learning from practice, this volume is an important and valuable contribution to the literature in the field.

Sally Brown
Pro-Vice-Chancellor, Assessment, Learning and Teaching and Professor of Diversity in Learning and Teaching in Higher Education
Leeds Metropolitan University.

Preface

It is increasingly the case that students' programs of study are not located within the confines of a single discipline area but rather are constructed to draw upon materials from several academic traditions.

There are three principal models of such programs:

- Joint honours degree or major / minor combinations in which the two subject areas are considered quite separately from each other.
- Multidisciplinary examples that draw separately from several disciplines to build up degrees with a number of components that retain their distinct disciplinary perspectives.
- Fully interdisciplinary programs in which elements from different disciplines are woven closely together to derive a wholly integrated approach to study.

Achievement of effective learning and teaching in the latter two of these models presents significant challenges over and above traditional discipline requirements and this is particularly so for interdisciplinary programs.

A key element in success is identified as the need for "give and take" and the acceptance of a blurring of intellectual and (in some instances) professional boundaries. Interprofessional education is becoming the de facto norm in several disciplines, such as nursing and medicine.

The volume provides a thorough consideration of the issues relating to the operation of interdisciplinary programs from both theoretical and practical perspectives. It takes as its principal objective the improvement of the quality of learning and teaching across interdisciplinary programs. However, throughout this practical objective has been considered within contemporary educational scholarship and research.

In conceptualizing and constructing this volume we have utilized a mix of horizontal and vertical metaphors:

- The horizontal matters are those that apply across the range of interdisciplinary programs regardless of academic themes addressed. These matters are covered in Part I.
- The vertical metaphor has been applied to a series of practitioner examples. These have been selected to give prominence to a variety of different approaches and different focused settings as used in specific fields of study. These matters are covered in Part II.

We have drawn on practice and experience from different countries. Whilst the majority of contributions are from U.K.-based contributors, the volume includes material from other locations to give an international "flavor" and relevance.

Dr Balasubramanyam Chandramohan and Dr Stephen Fallows

Acknowledgments

The editors would like to thank all authors who submitted/intended to submit their work. Unfortunately we could not accept all offers, but we will remain engaged with all for future work on interdisciplinarity.

Dr Balasubramanyam Chandramohan would also like to thank Texas A&M University (U.S.), Indian Institute of Science, Madurai Kamarajar University, and Mother Teresa Women's University (India) for their invitations to deliver guest lectures on different aspects of interdisciplinarity; and the U.K. Institute for Learning and Teaching in Higher Education (ILTHE) for a small grant that enabled him, among other activities, to carry out research at New York Public Library on interdisciplinarity and knowledge taxonomies in the U.S. He is also grateful to his colleagues and students at universities in Asia, Africa, Continental Europe, and the U.K. who shared his enthusiasm for interdisciplinarity in learning, teaching, and research.

Dr Fallows approaches interdisciplinarity from the perspective of a health scientist with a career that began with a degree in Nutrition (an interdisciplinary program of study) from the University of London through to his present position at the University of Chester. Interdisciplinary has been a constant. Recent work with M.Sc. students from around the world studying "Exercise and Nutrition Science," "Cardiovascular Rehabilitation," and "Weight Management" has confirmed his belief in the desirability of cross-discipline (and cross-profession) university education. Dr Fallows thanks all his Chester students for reconfirming his belief in the merits of interdisciplinary higher education.

I
Horizontal
Matters that Apply
across Entire Programs

1

"Problems May Cut Right across the Borders"
Why We Cannot Do Without Interdisciplinarity

R. J. ELLIS
University of Birmingham

Interdisciplinarity in higher education teaching has, since the mid-1970s, become ever more clearly defined. It is increasingly regarded as a learning mode involving the exploration of issues, problems, knowledge, and understanding through the integration and synthesis of theoretical or methodological procedures or both which draw upon more than one discipline and/or challenge conventional disciplinary approaches. Typically individuals or (more often) teams integrate information, techniques, perspectives, and/or concepts and theories from two or more disciplines or they develop or draw upon new alternatives.

Yet, despite efforts to become clearer about what the term means, a common verdict remains that interdisciplinary study is, in the words of Alan Liu, "the most seriously underthought critical, pedagogical and institutional concept in the modern academy" (Liu, 1989, p. 743). As Julie Klein puts it,

> interdisciplinarity has been variously defined . . . as a methodology, a concept, a process, a way of thinking, a philosophy, and a reflexive ideology. It has been linked with attempts to expose the dangers of fragmentation, to re-establish old connections, to explore emerging relations, and to create new subjects adequate to handle our practical and conceptual needs . . . [as] a means of solving problems and answering questions that cannot be satisfactorily addressed using single methods or approaches. (Klein, 1990, p. 196)

Perhaps then I need to start by saying that in this chapter I am not going to seek to resolve all these problems. It could be argued, *vis à vis* Klein, that interdisciplinarity is in fact all of the above, which makes it a complex beast. Faced with such multi-facetedness, it is, I think, still the case that developing interdisciplinary learning approaches usually proves to be daunting, and is especially challenging at the level of syllabus design, just because of a continuing level of "underthinking" concerning what exactly interdisciplinarity might constitute and entail. Liu's comment highlights how difficult it is to teach

3

interdisciplinarily, just because the very concept of what it might be remains somewhat "underthought."

Nevertheless, it has long seemed no more than plain common sense to seek to link up the different, supposedly separate, "discrete" disciplines and explore their interstices—the "spaces" in between them, simply because we do not experience our humanity or the world in terms of separate disciplines and can never understand our existence or environment in such a discipline-based way; we cannot think so fragmentedly in our day-to-day experience. So the issue of how to seek to stitch things together has to be addressed in a way going beyond the mere invocation of the word. Consequently it can be argued that:

> Interdisciplinary thinking is rapidly becoming an integral feature of research as a result of four powerful "drivers": the inherent complexity of nature and society, the desire to explore problems and questions that are not confined to a single discipline, the need to solve societal problems, and the power of new technologies. (COSEPUP, 2004, p. 2)

Another reason why the task is important is an instrumental one. More and more often various governmental and quasi-autonomous funding bodies that exist have expressed an interest in supporting the development of inter-disciplinary research: for example, in the U.K. this is true of the three government-funded Research Councils plus the Leverhulme Trust, and the Wellcome Trust. Indeed, by now innumerable successful interdisciplinary research projects have been established and in important respects inter-disciplinary research activity is flourishing. As academics come to invest more and more of their intellectual energies in such work, the expectation must be that this approach will extend more and more often to their teaching engagements as well. Therefore the need to be clear about what the concept constitutes and involves is obviously important at this time.

When approaching this task, it is perhaps still necessary to begin, as it were, at the beginning. Though arguments for an integrative approach to research and learning have been advanced from Plato through von Humboldt, the term "interdisciplinary" as it is generally understood today probably originated in the early decades of the twentieth century. Firstly there were the scientific stud-ies of the Vienna Circle on the philosophy of science from 1907 onwards, which sought to bring the clarification of philosophy—through the method of logical analysis—to the examination of all problems and assertions (drawing heavily on Wittgenstein). This scientific world-conception of the Vienna Circle is char-acterized "essentially by *two features. First* it is empricist and positivist [. . . and] *Second,* the scientific world-conception is marked by the application of a certain method, namely logical analysis" (Sarkar, 1996, p. 331). However, though its integrationist impulses meant that it did indeed seek to cross over the spaces between disciplines, the Vienna Circle never seems to have used the word "interdisciplinary."

Perhaps a little surprisingly, it was instead the social sciences that coined the term. It might have been anticipated that the term "interdisciplinary" would find its origins in the sciences, since these have always pursued research drawing on more than one discipline:

> The history of science from the time of the earliest scholarship abounds with examples of the integration of knowledge from many research fields. The pre-Socratic philosopher Anaximander brought together his knowledge of geology, paleontology, and biology to discern that living beings develop from simpler to more complex forms. In the age of the great scientific revolutions of 17th-century Europe, its towering geniuses—Isaac Newton, Robert Hooke, Edmond Halley, Robert Boyle, and others—brought their curiosity to bear not only on subjects that would lead to basic discoveries that bear their names but also on every kind of interdisciplinary challenge, including military and mining questions. In the 19th century, Louis Pasteur became a model interdisciplinarian, responding to practical questions about diseases and wine spoilage with surprising answers that laid the foundations of microbiology and immunology. (COSEPUP, 2004, p. 17)

Despite this, the term "interdisciplinar[it]y" seems to have been first used within the portals of the United States' Social Science Research Council. In the 1920s, documents produced by the Social Science Research Council, as part of the development of "A Constructive Program for the SSRC," mention the SSRC's desire to foster research "which brings in more than one discipline" (Robert Sessions Woodworth, quoted in Frank, 1988, p. 91; Klein, 1990, pp. 19–25).

Perhaps these early twentieth-century origins within the Vienna Circle and the U.S.'s SSRC are unsurprising. The Vienna Circle's work was an "endeavour . . . to link and harmonise the achievements of individual investigators in their various fields of science" (Sarkar, 1996, p. 328) and as such was an endeavor to establish a synthetic approach to the growing complexities of scientific enquiry. This burgeoning complexity meant that "big pictures" became harder and harder to arrive at. The Vienna Circle's goal, therefore, was "unified science" (Sarkar, 1996, p. 328). A similar burgeoning of the constituent disciplines within the social sciences was occurring at more or less the same time. The social sciences were rapidly widening in scope, leading, for example, to Margaret Mead calling in 1931 for "co-operation, for cross-fertilization in the social sciences." Here, the objective is more to do with the idea of exploring the "inter-"—the spaces between disciplines—and less on what might be described as the Vienna Circle's ontological and metasynthetic motivations.

Since these tentative beginnings in the early decades of the twentieth century, use of both the concept of interdisciplinarity and the word itself has rapidly grown, especially in the latter quarter of the twentieth century and the opening decade of the twenty-first. But the Vienna Circle's desire to seek unifi-cation and the SSRC's desire to establish links between disciplines perhaps illustrate two main thrusts hidden within the term "interdisciplinarity." Firstly, there is, recurrently, a desire to attain a universality which, this approach's advocates argue, is impeded by the fragmentation resulting from discipline-based approaches. Secondly there is a desire to search out what might be called "interdisciplines"—modes of enquiry moving between the frames of the estab-lished disciplines, def[r]aming their supposed adequacy. This latter can be represented conservatively as "conjunctive interaction" (Cluck, 1980, p. 67) or—more radically—as an entirely new mode of systemic conceptualization. I think it can be argued that searches for a metanarrative of conceptual enquiry have somewhat ebbed away, bruised by the assault of post-structuralist theori-zations, with their mistrust of such "meta" aspirations (Lyotard, 1979). Instead, priority is placed upon seeking modes of exploring the interstices and gaps between disciplines—their liminal thresholds, as they might be called—that reconfigure and at the same time destabilize the disciplines themselves.

The appealingly radical sound of this endeavor—an upset of the organ-ization of the academy—can in turn be related to the ructions in the social sciences and humanities in the late 1960s and the way these subsequently led to reconsiderations of the relationship between power and knowledge. Such reconsiderations also—arguably relatedly—stemmed in important respects from the development of a whole range of sociologies in the mid-twentieth century (of knowledge, of literature, of power, of gender, of the sciences, etc.). These sociological forays into the other disciplines demanded that inter-disciplinary consideration be extended, as academics in the sciences, human-ities, and the social sciences encountered and interacted with their sociological counterparts. The widespread educational disruptions of 1968 (in Paris, London, the U.S., and elsewhere) intensified this trend towards revolution-ary redefinition, aimed as it was (at least in part) at the academy (including its constituent discipline-based departments) and characterized as it was by an impatience with what was seen as a general institutional conservatism—manifested most plainly in a failure to resist the perceived injustices of this period. Certainly this provides one way of understanding how it was that var-ieties of political, social, and (subsequently) cultural theory came to such prominence at this time. In particular, humanities academics became engaged in often bruising but always productive exchanges with social scientists, leading to the importation of new modes of theorization, often embracing interdisciplinary concepts and concerns.

This set of revolutionary endeavors, sponsored by 1960s radicalism, radical sociologists, and the interface between them, might be described as the roman-tic discourse of interdisciplinary enquiry. For a time this approach helped render interdisciplinary work highly attractive, occurring as it did during a period of some social unrest. Indeed, arguably, this sort of radical appeal lingers on into the twenty-first century. When Roberta Frank in 1988 argued that " 'Interdisciplinary' has something to please everyone . . . the Latinate *discipline* comes encased in stainless steel; it suggests something rigorous, aggressive, hazardous to master; *Inter* hints that knowledge is . . . warm, mutually developing, consultative" she is ironically alluding to this enduring radical, communitarian appeal (Frank, 1988, p. 100). Or, as Tony Bennett put it in an enjoyable pun, interdisciplinarity can break out from the disciplines' inherent "disciplining" of thought (Bennett, 1998).[1] However, it can be argued that any such stress upon interdisciplinarity's reforming, innovative, and progressive potential—getting beyond the discipline's "disciplining"—worked to the disadvantage of the approach by helping to keep the term nebulous (and so more romantically appealing). Consequently in 1980 Cluck could complain with some legitimacy that "much of the discourse which purports to be interdisciplinary betrays a soft foundation which gives way under probing" (Cluck, 1980, p. 87).

Importantly, however, and increasingly often, the idea of interdisciplinarity has moved away from being colored by such a romantic representation and its accentuation of what might be called the "soft" connotations of the term. Instead interdisciplinarity has become invested by discourses articulating a general requirement for exploration of new areas of potential knowledge and discovery and proposing that certain problems were particularly amenable to interdisciplinary research (Maasen, 2000, p. 174). This is true in the humanities and social sciences, yet even more true in the sciences, where scientific and technological advances, accelerated by Second World War and Cold War research, opened up the possibilities of new kinds of conjunctive research between physics and the other sciences in particular at first, and then biological science and the other sciences in close succession, as well as between all of these and engineering.

This was a process depending upon a more rigorous understanding of what interdisciplinary work constitutes. Consequently, an important first step in apprehending this development depends upon drawing up distinctions between multidisciplinarity, interdisciplinarity, and disciplinarity in research and teaching. Multidisciplinary study involves employing two or more disciplines in juxtaposition. But "these separate disciplines never intersect upon a well-defined matrix" (Cluck, 1980, p. 68). Instead the process of research and learning is additive (Klein, 1990, p. 56). By contrast, interdisciplinary work is integrationist and consultative. Though, of course, "there is some overlap between interdisciplinary and multidisciplinary study," nevertheless "for the most part they are different areas" (Kline, 1995, p. 2). Interdisciplinary work is much more firmly rooted in "conjunctive interaction" (Cluck, 1980, p. 68; Klein, 2000, p. 56). The approach is synthetic (the prefix "inter-" requiring a degree of synthesizing) (Kline, 1995, p. 2), and hinges upon the establishment of a central focus (conceptual, theoretical, and/or methodological).

Arguably this sort of interaction became easier in the late twentieth century, as the pressure of increasing amounts of interdisciplinary work ensured that discipline boundaries became more blurred in the sciences, the social sciences, and the humanities (Klein, 2000, p. 7). Hence, understanding interdisciplinarity demands an understanding of its relationship to disciplinarity.

When drawing up this distinction between discipline-based and interdisciplinary work, a starting point is the idea that disciplinary exploration depending upon identifying a category of knowledge which can be conventionally identified as belonging to that discipline. A discipline may therefore be defined as "a specific body of teachable knowledge with its own background of education, training, procedures, methods and content areas" (Berger, 1970). Such a definition is perhaps both too narrow, for it offers no sense of the dynamism of each and every discipline's evolution, and too wide, needing to be more specific about how "procedures and methods" might be effectively differentiated (Gozzer, 1982, p. 286). Yet, as a definition it is helpful, because it suggests how both multidisciplinary and interdisciplinary approaches might work. Where multidisciplinary approaches draw separately upon the existing disciplines' own methods and procedures (alongside one another, with, broadly, any bridging not being explicit), interdisciplinary work explicitly seeks to integrate or establish "interdisciplinary" methods and procedures (effecting some sort of bridging or synthesis). But such a distinction also, inevitably, raises the issue of the appropriate relationship of the disciplines to each other and to the larger intellectual terrain in which these disciplines are located (Kline, 1995, p. 2).

Considering these "territorial" issues has been termed the study of "disciplinarity" (Messer-Davidow et al., 1993). This defining of the discipline and its ("unique") methods and procedures has long been a feature of most disciplines' syllabi at some point. But increasingly such self-reflexive examinations highlight how the establishment of such genealogies (between disciplines) sets up boundaries—"borders"—that must be identified as relative and not essential, even as they are patrolled. Specifically, this is because disciplines are also social structures, "organizations made up of human beings with vested interests based on time investments, acquired reputations, and established social networks that shape and bias their views on the relative importance of their knowledge" (Weingert & Stehr, 2000, p. xi). Taking up this position leads to the emergence of radical (post-structuralist) definitions of disciplines (see, for example, Turner, 2000, p. 47).

Such critiques of disciplinarity suggest that whilst the discipline-based approach has clear conceptual advantages (of clarity and capacity for specialized study), it is also limiting. There is always the possibility of substantial omission if knowledge is wholly structured within disciplines (Campbell, 1969), not least because prevailing disciplinary arrangements have never been more than a marriage of convenience in which the elements of academia were never smoothly united on the basis of general agreement (Graff, 1987). As Karl

Popper puts it, "We are not students of some subject matter, but students of problems. And problems may cut right across the borders of any subject matter or discipline" (Popper, 1963, p. 88).

Interdisciplinary work, in one of its key configurations, can therefore explore those arenas of knowledge—those liminal threshold areas—outside of the disciplines, "betwixt and between," as Victor Turner puts it (Turner, 1987), so establishing such work in a liminal area that is, as it were, "neither the one nor the other" (Turner, 1977). In other words, interdisciplinary work comprehends that disciplines, because of their need to establish and preserve distinctions between themselves, may leave some areas of knowledge relatively under-explored or even completely unexplored.

Arguably, however, in the late twentieth century, all discipline boundaries became increasingly blurred by overlaps—such as those created by sociology, or by cultural studies, or by the multiplication of "bio-s"—biochemistry, biophysics, bioengineering, and biogeochemistry, etc. (COSEPUP, 2004, p. 18; Klein, 2000, p. 7). Hence, understanding interdisciplinarity demands an understanding of its relationship to disciplinarity, just because interdisciplinary work, in seeking to integrate, seeks to establish "*interdisciplinary*" methods and procedures.

Such a recognition also suggests that whilst discipline-based approaches have clear conceptual advantages (by offering clarity and the capacity for specialized study), they may also be limiting. Dividing study up into separate disciplines may have been around since Aristotle's *Metaphysics* (at least). Yet Aristotle himself saw such divisions as regrettable, if necessary. And the recurrent claim has been—as for example, when advanced by José Ortega y Gasset—that the progressive compartmentalization of knowledge into specialisms at the expense of more all-embracing approaches led to the "learned ignoramus . . . a person who is ignorant, not in the fashion of the ignorant man, but with all the petulance of one who is learned in his own special line" (Ortega y Gasset, 1930, p. 112). Joe Moran points out how this sort of analysis carries a trace of elitism in it—an elitism even more obvious in the case of Nietzsche (Moran, 2002, p. 13). But it also draws attention to the way that ignorance can result from resting within discrete disciplinary boundaries—ignorance of what may lie in the interstices between disciplines, or beyond them. Undoubtedly the discipline-specific approach, whatever its shortcomings, can still sustain itself because it is institutionalized and can draw therefore on institutions' capacities self-perpetuatingly to reproduce themselves. Yet the risk is that species of ignorance can thereby fester, and, indeed, proliferate in the face of ever-accelerating new developments in humanity, the world, and their interaction.

In this argument, interdisciplinary work in one of its key configurations can potentially—at the very least—explore those areas of knowledge and understanding that disciplines, because of their need to establish and preserve distinctions between themselves, may leave relatively or utterly unexplored.

However, such an emphasis reveals one of the difficulties of interdisciplinary undertakings. It can be argued that interdisciplinary work, relying as it does upon an understanding of the disciplines with which it "inter-disciplines," has to be primarily or even wholly a post-graduate, even post-doctoral undertaking, in which "experts" understand "the relationship of their particular discipline to other disciplines and the totality of human knowledge" (Kline, 1995, p. 4). Indeed, with comic intent, the experience of undertaking an interdisciplinary project has been described as going through ten stages before it can get off the ground. I myself recall pretty much going through these stages back in the 1960s: singing the old songs (that is to say, rehearsing one's own disciplinary understandings); believing everyone on the other side is an idiot (for having understandings that are differently constituted); retreating into abstractions (by offering the other side your disciplinary conceptual fundaments); experiencing definition sickness (discovering differences of definition); jumping the tussocks (finding one or two isolated points of agreement and trying to progress on this basis); playing the glass bead game (trying to lay foundations via exchanges); experiencing the great failure (finding one cannot agree on these foundations); asking "what is happening to me?" (as finally one begins to question one's own disciplinary assumptions and recognizes their arbitrariness and conventionality); and getting to know the enemy (actually working to understand and bridge). It is only after all these nine stages that the tenth stage, "the real beginning", is arrived at (Sjölander, 1985). I think Sjölander's entertaining scenario is, however, by now largely past its sell-by date. One of the encouraging signs of how interdisciplinary modes of thinking have penetrated the academy is that most academics coming together now just do not generally plod through these nine stages. Nor is there any need for their students to do this. I would argue, for example, that post-structuralism has generally put paid to Sjölander's taxonomy: discipline-based scholars have already been taught to be self-reflexive: to critique their own practices self-consciously. So they are not so readily flummoxed when faced with those coming to their discipline from outside perspectives.

What is still needed is clarity about what (and how much) is being attempted as one begins. Different levels of ambition can be defined. For example, some interdisciplinary work can now draw upon a substantial set of procedures and theories that have attained a measure of self-sufficiency. In this, a set of salient concepts has been identified, assembled, and deployed (as, for example, in psycholinguistics, biochemistry, and queer studies). Having such supports to hand makes the starting-up of study in these fields relatively unproblematic. But in other cases, the groundwork is far less established and much more is consequently being bitten off.

Plainly, when thinking along these lines, it quickly becomes apparent that there is a need to recognise decisive qualitative differences between types of interdisciplinary studies. Such studies may:

- Develop conceptual links using a perspective in one discipline to modify a perspective in another discipline;
- Recognize a new level of organization with its own processes in order to solve unsolved problems within existing disciplines or problems that lie beyond the scope of any one discipline;
- Use research techniques developed in one discipline to elaborate a theoretical model in another;
- Modify and extend a theoretical framework from one domain to apply in another;
- Develop a new theoretical framework that may reconceptualize research in separate domains as it attempts to integrate them;
- Address broad issues and/or complex questions spanning more than one disciplinary field. (William Bechtel, 1986, pp. 46–7; Klein, 1990, p. 11)

As the U.S.'s Committee on Science, Engineering, and Public Policy (COSEPUP) dryly notes, "it may take extra time for building consensus and for learning new methods, languages, and cultures" (COSEPUP, 2004, p. 3).

What certainly seems to be the case is that, because the coverage of disciplines is incomplete and partial (in both senses of the word), some migration of specialisms and some hybridization is inevitable. Linguistics' interactions with the (other) social sciences certainly fully demonstrates this, with psycholinguistics, sociolinguistics, and chemical engineering in particular firmly established as what can be called interdisciplines—areas of knowledge, study, and learning with distinct, evolving theoretical and methodological procedures—in this sense, definitively neither the one discipline or the other discipline (or other disciplines). More such established interdisciplines can readily now be named: gender studies; postcolonial studies; biochemical engineering, etc. Some of these may even be mutating into disciplines, like cultural studies—though, in the latter case, any such mutation is certainly reluctant since, as part of its conceptual fundaments, cultural studies has always insisted upon its political awareness—and as such is suspicious still of any institutionalization. Such more-or-less established interdisciplines are certainly not unamenable to undergraduate study. What can also be seen is that different kinds of interdisciplinary endeavor have different degrees of ambitiousness. One of my central claims today is that distinctions between these different levels of interdisciplinary ambition need to be drawn up before any attempt to teach interdisciplinarily can become viable. One needs, as it were, to provide the student with the resources of an interdiscipline, or show the student what these are, but it also means that each interdiscipline needs to be defined in terms of its particular set of theoretical and methodological procedures. Another of my central claims today is that this does not need to be as daunting to the tutor or the learner as this formulation might make it sound.

However, it is crucial that such a framework is provided, else so-called inter-disciplinary work will more than likely end up by "fall[ing] back upon" a "default" position relying upon a "discipline-based perspective," in which any links between the disciplines predominantly are left to take place in the students' minds (Klein, 1990, pp. 25, 56). Yet it is also important that things do not become too purist at this point, else the recurrence of words such as "difficulties," "problems," "pitfalls," and "unclear" in the titles of studies of interdisciplinarity (Gozzer, 1982; Sjölander, 1985) will ultimately prove to be all too explicable and discouraging. I think that when Stanley Fish writes in "Being Interdisciplinary Is So Very Hard to Do" that what is involved in interdisciplinarity is the establishment of theoretical "metadisciplines," he is actually depending on such purist arguments (Fish, 1994). And he does indeed make things sound very daunting.

One way of proceeding to answer this question of how this "inter-" can work in a less daunting way is to begin to identify certain theories and/or approaches and/or skills that are not specific to a single discipline, but are taken up—perhaps in different ways and with different emphases—by more than one discipline, or by an interdiscipline. And one way of thinking about these theories, approaches, and skills is to apply to them something like the label "transferable interdisciplinary methods." Transferable interdisciplinary methods may be able to be identified that can help lubricate points of interdisciplinary conjunction. This suggestion gains particular weight in the humanities in the terrains of contextualization and historicization: the foregrounding of cultural and/or political theorizations can be of particular value in these arenas.

An example might be some aspects of the theories of Foucault to do with discourse. These were taken up strongly in cultural studies in the latter third of the twentieth century, and in the same moment, more broadly in the arts and humanities in some styles of textual study. Foucault's theories also increasingly came to be deployed in the social sciences (unsurprisingly, given the emphasis of his work). Using Foucault can help identify how common ideological concerns are articulated *discursively* in different disciplinary terrains, in more or less different but related ways. In this sense a Foucauldian approach might be described as a transferable interdisciplinary method that derives not necessarily from the disciplines immediately to hand, but suggested by the issues and problems that are confronted. Other methods can be derived from gender studies, queer studies, postcolonial studies, post-Marxist studies, and post-structuralist explorations.

Let me provide at this point an example: border theorizations of space, place, and contact, that draw upon post-Marxist, postcolonial, and post-structural theorizations—for example, those of Henri Lefebvre to do with how space is never empty or neutral but always the space of social practices (Lefebvre, 1991). One consequence of this has been an exploration of the contention that the imperialist-tending, ethnic-specific territorial imagination is becoming increasingly superseded in a process of deterritorialization. The focus is shifting from concentration upon double-"o" "ro*o*ts" to an idea of "o" plus "u": "ro*o*ts: ro*u*tes," with space increasingly mapped out in flows. Focus falls upon movement, crossings, types of circulation, as manifested, for example, in Gloria Anzaldúa's *Borderlands/La Frontera: The new mestiza.* Thus *Borderlands* is dedicated "To you who walked with me upon my path . . ./ to you who brushed past me at crossroads" (Anzaldúa, 1987, p. vii). Indeed, Anzaldúa celebrates and warns of the dangers of such movement: "a border culture in a constant state of transition . . . The prohibited and forbidden are its inhabitants. Los atravesados live there . . . those who cross over, pass over or go through the confines of the 'normal' . . . transgressors, aliens" (Anzaldúa, 1987, p. 3).

At stake in these tensions within Anzaldúa's *Borderlands/La Frontera* are issues of space and spatialization—the way space is conceptualized, and acculturated as space. Static understandings of nation state come under stress. It is of course true that national borders have not yet, by any means, dissolved, but " '*border studies*' of the intersections and interactions of different cultures of the United States" can, it is argued, give a better understanding of an ever more globalizing space of cultural, social, and political exchange, and of migration, asylum, and population movement. In all this, Mary Louise Pratt's concept of "contact zones" has come very much to the fore. Pratt demystifies the contact zone—that arena of cultural contact, exchange, and often domination and oppression—making it over into a process of material social and cultural conflict. Pratt's particular focus has been what she described as autoethnographic texts—texts "in which people undertake to describe themselves in ways that engage with representations others have of them . . . involv[ing] . . . selective collaboration with and appropriation". As Pratt points out, this is a process of "transculturation"—a process whereby members of "subordinated or marginal groups select and invent from materials transmitted to them by a dominant . . . culture" (Pratt, 1992, p. 6; Pratt, 1999, p. 589).[2]

Under these sorts of arguments, edges and margins have come to assume considerable—even definitive—significance in cultural criticism. Processes of marginalization, in which minorities have been largely or entirely excluded from power, have been considered in relationship to processes of oppositional multicultural and intercultural exchange—both by way of diasporic negotiation and by way of hybrid borderland encounters. These ideas, drawing upon the work of Homi Bhabha, Gayatri Spivak, and other postcolonial theorists, underpin Pratt's formulation of the idea of the contact zone as a testing field of fluid transcultural exchange.

Transferable interdisciplinary methods like these may be able to be identified that can help lubricate points of interdisciplinary conjunction: in this instance the interdisciplinary methods can be used to highlight how cultural relativism plays a significant part in any understanding of "place" and "space."

All this is not to say that, at its most demanding, interdisciplinary endeavors cannot become less well suited for undergraduate study. A case in point is when interdisciplinary work becomes "transdisciplinary," evolving its own synthetic, encompassing amalgams of other disciplines' theories and methods as it searches for unifying and comprehensive comprehension of problems and issues (Klein, 1990, pp. 66–71) (and even though even these transdisciplinary moments—quite rightly—remain of considerable appeal to undergraduates).

Furthermore, I also think one needs to be wary in all this. COSEPUP may be prepared to enthuse that "Despite frequent tensions over budgets, space, and intellectual turf, many of these centers and institutes are vibrant research and training environments. They do not supersede the departments but complement them, often generating new kinds of excitement" (COSEPUP, 2004, p. 18), but just possibly COSEPUP is here glossing over the budgetary tensions for strategic reasons. Often, these budgetary issues are constitutive: there is just no escape from the bottom line. Maybe, even, budgetary considerations underlie governmental and institutional enthusiasm for interdisciplinary institutes. There is a growing argument that the current institutional enthusiasm for interdisciplinary work, espoused as it is now by so many higher education institutions and so frequently lauded as it is by both governmental and quasi-autonomous funding bodies, is indicative of a decidedly dark underside to the synthetic revolution. In this argument, as advanced for example by Bill Readings, interdisciplinary initiatives are seen as a cut-price means of being flexible in the academic marketplace—providing a means of responding to new demand[s] (Readings, 1996). As Hal Foster points out, this approach (setting up "institutes" rather than something more concretely located in institutional terms) can make interdisciplinarity very cost-effective (Foster, 1998). Not least this is because, as Vincent B. Leitch observes, there is no need to establish an expensive new Academic Department with all of the established infrastructural supports that such a measure entails; rather "institutes" can be cut according to the cloth available (Leitch & Ruiz, 2005). Academics can work, as it were, double time: inside their departments and within the interdisciplinary institute.

This is just one aspect of a set of problems needing to be addressed, which COSEPUP identified in 2004:

> In attempting to balance the strengthening of disciplines and the pursuit of interdisciplinary research, education, and training, many institutions are impeded by traditions and policies that govern hiring, promotion, tenure, and resource allocation. . . . The increasing specialization and cross-fertilizations in science and engineering require new modes of organization and a modified reward structure to facilitate interdisciplinary interactions. . . . Professional societies have the opportunity to facilitate IDR by producing state-of-the-art reports on recent

research developments and on curriculum, assessment, and accreditation methods; enhancing personal interactions; building partnerships among societies; publishing interdisciplinary journals and special editions of disciplinary journals; and promoting mutual understanding of disciplinary methods, languages, and cultures.... Reliable methods for prospective and retrospective evaluation of interdisciplinary research and education programs will require modification of the peer-review process to include researchers with interdisciplinary expertise in addition to researchers with expertise in the relevant disciplines. (COSEPUP, 2004, p. 3)

The risk in not confronting the last two of these problems is that what will result for students is intellectual indiscipline, if you will excuse the pun, as students "fall into an eclecticism that does little work" and which is therefore "more entropic than transgressive" (Foster, 1998, p. 162).

Perhaps then we should take more careful note of how, commonly, in the sciences there is a strong stress placed upon the importance of establishing foundational theoretical and methodological training in students as a first step, before more adventurous interdisciplinary work is undertaken. When I interviewed a physicist here at Birmingham University about his interdisciplinary work, he mentioned on at least five occasions the need for the students to have a broad set of mathematical skills; with each iteration he was at the same time establishing that shortcuts were hard to come by in an interdisciplinary approach. Foundations have to be carefully laid, and tutors need to have a clear sense of what that foundational set is, how it needs to be taught, and what resources are needed to support it. This is something I would very much concur with, and perhaps it is a note on which to end this chapter. Interdisciplinary learning cannot but be demanding, though it does not need to be daunting, as the skills set and/or salient concepts the interdiscipline needs is acquired or re-articulated. And what can then happen is that liminal arenas can be opened up for the student, which are indeed "betwixt and between" and "neither the one nor the other"—arenas that the student can see can dramatically contribute to human knowledge in new ways. Interdisciplinary approaches can indeed have a transformative potential, which is surely why students are so strongly drawn towards them. There is little doubt, for example, that students realize that pressing global problems, from intercontinental social inequalities to climate change, are best addressed by interdisciplinary approaches. Approaching such macro problems as these, or more micro ones (for example to do with particular technological, scientific, or cultural or social problems) in an interdisciplinary way inevitably entails representing to the students that they are seekers after knowledge and allowing them the freedom to carry out such quests. This, above all, is what interdisciplinary teaching should, and must involve. And it must be properly resourced in order to do this.

Notes

1. To explain the pun: disciplining can be taken to involve some form of castiga-
tion—typically involving corporal punishment; on the other hand, disciplining
can be read more positively, as a means of providing and/or sustaining a clear
framework of order and stability (as in self-discipline).
2. In some ways, "transculturation," at least until recently, is one way of character-
izing what interdisciplinarians have had to effect when treating with the disciplines with which they seek to interact.

References

Anzaldúa, Gloria. (1987). *Borderlands/La Frontera: The new mestiza*. San Francisco: Spinsters/Aunt
Lute.
Bechtel, W. (Ed.) (1986). *Integrating scientific disciplines*. Dordrecht: Martinus Nijhoff.
Bennett, T. (1998). *Culture: A reformer's science*. London: Sage.
Berger, G. (1970). Introduction. *OECD-CERI interdisciplinarity—Problems of teaching and research
in universities*. Nice: CERI/French Ministry of Education.
Campbell, D. (1969). Ethnocentrism of disciplines and the fish-scale model of omniscience. In M.
Sherif and C. Sherif (Eds.), *Interdisciplinary relationships in the social sciences* (pp. 328–348).
Chicago: Aldine.
Cluck, N. A. (1980). Reflections on the interdisciplinary approach to the humanities. *Liberal Educa-
tion, 66*(1), 67–77.
Committee on Science, Engineering, and Public Policy (COSEPUP) (2004). *Facilitating inter-
disciplinary research*. Washington: COSEPUP. Retrieved November 15, 2006, from http://
fermat.nap.edu/books/0309094356/html/27.html.
Fish, S. (1994). *There's no such thing as free speech, and it's a good thing, too*. New York: Oxford
University Press.
Foster, H. (1998). Trauma studies and the interdisciplinary: An overview. In Alex Coles and Alexia
Defert (Eds.), *The anxiety of interdisciplinarity* (pp. 157–168). London: BACKless Books.
Frank, R. (1988). Interdisciplinary: The first half-century. In E. G. Stanley and T. F. Hoad (Eds.),
Words: for Robert Burchfield's sixty-fifty birthday (pp. 91–102). Woodbridge: Boydell and
Brewer.
Gozzer, G. (1982). Interdisciplinarity: A concept still unclear. *Prospects, 12*(3), 281–292.
Graff, G. (1987). *Professing literature*. Chicago: University of Chicago Press.
Klein, J. T. (1999). *Mapping interdisciplinary studies*. Washington, DC: Association of American
Colleges and Universities. http://www.is. wayne.edu/jklein/.
Klein, J. T. (2000). A conceptual vocabulary of interdisciplinary science. In Weingart and Stehr
(pp. 3–24).
Kline, S. J. (1995). *Conceptual foundations for multidisciplinary thinking*. Stanford, CA: Stanford
University Press.
Lefebvre, H. (1991). *The production of space*. Trans. David Nicholson-Smith. Oxford: Blackwell.
Leitch, V. B., and Ruiz, N. III (2005). Theory, interdisciplinarity and the humanities today:
An interview with Vincent B. Leitch. *InterCulture 2* (May), 1–14. http://www.fsu.edu/
%7Eproghum/interculture/VBL%20Interview.htm. Accessed 07 August 2005.
Liu, A. (1989). The power of formalism: The new historicism, *ELH: English Literary History, 56*(4)
(Winter), 721–771.
Lyotard, J.-F. (1979). *The postmodern condition: A report on knowledge* (Reprint ed.). Trans. Geoff
Bennington and Brian Massumi. Minneapolis: University of Minnesota Press.
Maasen, S. (2000). Inducing interdisciplinarity. In Weingart and Stehr (pp. 173–193).
Messer-Davidow, E., Shumway, D. R., and Sylvan, D. J. (1993). *Knowledges: Historical and critical
studies in disciplinarity*. Charlottesville: University Press of Virginia.
Moran, J. (2002). *Interdisciplinarity*. London: Routledge.
Ortega y Gasset, J. (1930). *The revolt of the masses* (Reprinted 1957). New York: Norton.
Popper, K. R. (1963). *Conjectures and refutations: The growth of scientific knowledge*. New York:
Routledge and Kegan Paul.
Pratt, M. L. (1992). *Imperial eyes: Studies in travel writing and transculturation*. London: Routledge.
Pratt, M. L. (1999). Arts of the Contact Zone. In D. Bartholmae and A. Petrosky (Eds.), *Ways of
reading* (pp. 581–595). New York: Bedford St. Martins.

Readings, B. (1996). *The university in ruins.* Cambridge, MA: Harvard University Press.

Sarkar, S. (1996). *The emergence of logical empiricism: From 1900 to the Vienna Circle.* New York: Garland Publishing.

Sjölander, S. (1985). Long-term and short-term interdisciplinary work: Difficulties, problems and pitfalls. In L. Levin and I. Lind (Eds.), *Interdisciplinarity revisited* (pp. 85–101). Stockholm: OECD, SNBUC, Linköping University.

Turner, S. (2000). What are disciplines? And how is interdisciplinarity different? In Weingart and Stehr (pp. 46–65).

Turner, V. (1977). *The Ritual Process: Structure and Anti-Structure.* Ithaca, NY: Cornell University Press.

Turner, V. (1987). Betwixt and between: The liminal period in rites of passage. In C. Mahdi, S. Foster, and M. Little (Eds.), *Betwixt and between: Patterns of masculine and feminine initiation* (pp. 3–19). La Salle, IL: Open Court.

Weingart, P., and Stehr, N. (2000). *Practising interdisciplinarity*, Toronto: University of Toronto Press.

2

Ethics of Interdisciplinarity
Theory and Practice

SUSAN ILLINGWORTH

University of Leeds

Introduction

The requirement to teach ethics is on the increase throughout Higher Education (HE). The majority of QAA Benchmarking Statements makes reference to moral issues or concerns and most professional associations now expect some level of ethical awareness in their graduate entrants. Accordingly, many departments whose main academic interests lie elsewhere are making room within their curricula for an introduction to the moral skills and issues germane to their area of expertise. This area of learning will be designated "professional ethics" for the purposes of the following discussion.

When ethics is taught within humanities-based disciplines such as philosophy, it is presented as a body of knowledge to be subjected to conceptual analysis and critical appraisal, and does not normally include learning objectives defined in terms of expected changes in the students' values, character, or behaviour. In this respect it contrasts markedly with professional ethics, for whether professional ethics emphasizes professionalism, fitness for practice, or an acquaintance with morally contentious aspects of the parent discipline, it is taught on the assumption that students will need to use and act on what they have learned in real life. This is not to say that professional ethics courses cannot be structured around the study of moral philosophy but rather, that the study of moral philosophy in this context is used as a means to the end of shaping professional character and behaviour.

The cross-disciplinary nature of professional ethics raises important questions regarding the basis of its commonality. Does ethics arise in an otherwise diverse range of faculties and departments because it is generic, supradisciplinary, or interdisciplinary? This chapter will argue that all three of the above categories would be relevant to an overview of the role of professional ethics within HE, but that interdisciplinarity poses new challenges that merit special attention. An outline of the generic and supradisciplinary aspects of professional ethics will be offered first, to distinguish them from ethics as an interdisciplinary area of enquiry. Interdisciplinary ethics will then be considered in more detail. Specifically, I shall ask whether there is a need for an ethics of interdiscipliniarity, as a distinct and separate sub-discipline within the broader framework of professional ethics.

Generic Aspects of Professional Ethics

The study of professional ethics teaches a number of transferable skills that can help students meet challenges that are likely to arise, whatever their future working environment. It does this by providing them with a way of addressing normative issues and value judgements. Professionals need to do more than decide what their options are and how those options can be put into practice: they must also decide what ought to be done. A student who has learned how to recognize, define, and justify value judgements will therefore be a more effective decision-maker than one who lacks these skills. A consideration of ethical issues can be of particular benefit within science-based subjects where the emphasis on implementation and problem-based learning means that students will otherwise have little opportunity to consider the values and principles inherent in the aims that structure their work.

Courses that teach professional ethics via the study of moral philosophy will also foster a reasoned, objective, and dispassionate approach to decision-making that is self-aware and self-critical. Moral philosophy does not focus on memorizing facts or procedures but on a way of thinking that is clear, structured, and methodical, and can be expected to develop the following intellectual faculties:

- Conceptual analysis: a capacity for clear and logical appraisal of complex issues;
- Flexibility and independence of mind: the ability to consider issues from multiple perspectives;
- Rational decision-making: the ability to make choices based on coherent principles of thought and action;
- Effective communication: the ability to express views clearly, both verbally and in writing.

The study of professional ethics will be of use within any program that aims to give students a broad educational base, but these generic aspects are essentially discipline-neutral rather than interdisciplinary, and do not suggest grounds for an ethics of interdisciplinarity.

Supradisciplinary Aspects of Professional Ethics

Ethics can be defined as supradisciplinary when it raises issues that are not generic, in that they arise from specifically moral concerns, but are nevertheless common to a wide range of otherwise unconnected disciplines.

A measure of supradisciplinarity should be expected given ethics' fundamental relevance to all aspects of human agency, both private and professional.

An agricultural scientist working in an environmentally sensitive location may have different moral priorities from those of a nurse specializing in the care of the terminally ill, but this does not mean that they must appeal to distinct or incommensurable sets of values. Similarly, while it may be reasonable to assume that a person *qua* professional might have different moral obligations to that same person *qua* private citizen this does not mean that they cannot justify their behaviour under both aspects by appeal to a consistent and coherent moral belief system. Indeed, whenever the target "audience" for these justifications is the general public, it is essential that any principles appealed to or arguments offered are capable of attracting a high degree of consensus.

There are many circumstances in which a professional may be required to show evidence of having given explicit consideration to the ethical implications of their work, such as:

- Use of human or animal experimental subjects;
- Environmental impact;
- Allocation of public resources;
- Access to confidential or sensitive information;
- Introduction/development of controversial science or technology;
- Impact on cultural or religious sensitivities;
- Impact on fellow employees' conditions of work.

The dangers of losing public confidence have been highlighted in recent years by a number of well-publicized scandals in science and medicine,[1] but these events took place against a background of an already changing relationship between public and professional. The Internet is a medium through which the public can gain access to a wealth of information. From official sources such as the Home Office's pages on the use of Animals in Scientific Procedures through the Research Councils and bodies such as the Nuffield Council on Bioethics to national and international campaigning organizations such as Greenpeace and the Worldwide Fund for Nature,[2] people can inform themselves on ethically sensitive matters and involve themselves in public debate more readily than ever before. Accordingly, many organizations and companies now see an overtly "moral" stance as an essential part of their public image, and even those who are less scrupulous must pay some heed to public opinion.

Shared features of ethical discourse within public life find their counterpart in cross-disciplinary themes in ethics learning and teaching, such as:

- Application of moral theory to professional practice;
- Discussion of contested moral issues from multiple perspectives;
- Informed consent;
- Confidentiality;
- Service-user/client autonomy;
- Sensitivity to cultural and religious concerns.

Supradisciplinary ethics learning and teaching prepares students to engage in debate on moral issues with people who do not share their professional perspective, be they from other professions or none. It does this by helping them to step aside from the values, priorities, perspectives, and interests of their own discipline in a search for common ground. It is not generic as the issues relate specifically to ethics rather than to general performance, but it is not interdisciplinary either, for it aims to provide the professional with a discourse framework that lies above (or at least outside) their own discipline.

Interdisciplinary Aspects of Professional Ethics

Ethics is interdisciplinary when it concerns interactions between people from more than one discipline in a context of which distinct disciplinary identities are an integral and necessary part rather than a source of bias to be set aside.

Despite the advantages of supradisciplinarity, professional ethics often focuses upon the distinguishing features of a given discipline or specialism. This does not mean that there are moral principles or values that are only "good" for students of that discipline, but rather that they apply differing emphases to supradisciplinary principles and values. For example, beneficence and respect for patient autonomy are both regarded as key duties within biomedical ethics (Beauchamp & Childress, 1994, p. 38) but when conflicts arise doctors and nurses often differ in the relative importance they ascribe to these principles, with nurses prioritizing patient autonomy and doctors placing greater emphasis on their obligation of beneficence (Robertson, 1996). Similarly, a study of in-hospital ethics seminars carried out by Alderson, Farsides, and Williams (2002) reported "the frequently discussed contrast between geneticists offering choice and other clinicians recommending best treatment."

Nursing and paramedical staff often spend more time with their patients than doctors, conversing with them in a way that goes beyond the medical details of the case, and this can influence their evaluation of such things as the patient's quality of life, or capacity to give informed consent. Discipline-specificity with respect to the observance of professional duties will often be reinforced by service-user expectations; for example, a client may want empathy and support from a counsellor, while requiring a solicitor to offer clear and authoritative advice. Professional roles, in so far as they define the terms and degree of contact with service-users, have a profound influence on the way in which supradisciplinary principles are interpreted and applied to daily working practice. Approaches to professional ethics that focus on the correlation between professional role and individual character traits or virtues (Oakley & Cocking, 2002) show similar discipline-relative variations in the weight attached to the professional virtues through which shared moral principles are expressed.

In contrast to this continuing evolution of individual professional moralities and virtues, the increasing prevalence of interdisciplinary or interprofessional working is leading to the development of cross-disciplinary models for moral decision-making. Malin, Wilmot and Beswick (2000) have noted that current government policy requires a much closer degree of harmonization across the primary health–social care boundary, and has accordingly increased the demand for professionals capable of working across organizational boundaries. The Learning and Teaching Support Network (LTSN) subject centre for Health Sciences and Practice recognized this need and commissioned a review to provide guidance to teachers engaged in interprofessional education (LTSN Subject Centre for Health Sciences and Practice, 2002).

There is a further, ethics-specific, impetus for an interdisciplinary approach in the increasing number of General Ethics Committees being set up in the United Kingdom. For example, the Southern Derbyshire Community NHS Trust Ethical Advisory Group includes members from clinical psychology, occupational therapy, speech and language therapy, physiotherapy, nursing, professional development, psychiatry, administration, operational management, and citizen advocacy, in addition to independent observers (Malin et al., 2000). Research Ethics Committees also draw their members from a range of disciplines, as do the ethics advisory committees of many professional associations and funding bodies. Effective performance by regulatory bodies of this type can only be achieved if each member is able to contribute their own discipline-based expertise within the context of a fully integrated interdisciplinary moral decision-making process.

Interdisciplinary Learning and Teaching

The extent to which interprofessional working practices are driving an increase in shared learning programmes is unclear but there are signs that HE is beginning to recognize the advantages of incorporating interdisciplinary education and training provision into pre-registration programs. The use of interdisciplinary learning as a means towards the end of greater interprofessional cooperation is not limited to ethical concerns but the Peach Report (Peach, 1999) concluded that the subjects seen to offer most scope for shared learning were ethics and communications skills (Peach, 1999, para. 5.39). A pilot study run by Edward and Preece (1999) examined shared teaching in ethics for nurses and medical students at the University of Dundee. They decided to start with ethics for a number of reasons, including:

- The potential for mutual support on ethical issues;
- The classes would help to establish a shared notion of "good" between doctors and nurses.

Learning objectives of this type are supradisciplinary rather than interdisciplinary, aiming to mitigate the interprofessional conflict that can arise from:

- Different perceptions of care;
- Different points of view concerning patients' best interests;
- Variations in professional value systems;
- Variations in moral reasoning processes (Edward & Preece, 1999).

However, interdisciplinarity can be advantageous within the learning and teaching environment even if the overall direction of the module is towards supradisciplinarity. For example, exposing students to different professional viewpoints can greatly improve the effectiveness of discussion-oriented learning (Tugcu et al. 1995) by helping to make hidden assumptions, embedded ideals, and implied value judgements more overt and explicit. Further, interdisciplinarity will facilitate a broader perspective on gender-sensitive issues when professional gender profiles would result in single-discipline classes being drawn predominantly from one sex. Interdisciplinary groups can also be used to explore attitudes to moral authority, addressing intra- and interprofessional hierarchies and their relevance to personal autonomy and responsibility.

For these and other reasons, teachers may choose to encourage students to explore individual professional moralities, even if their primary ethical learning objectives aspire to the creation of a shared perspective. However, the question remains as to whether there are reasons to extend interdisciplinarity beyond learning and teaching into the realm of professional ethical practice.

Interdisciplinary Professional Ethics

Against the adoption of an interdisciplinary approach, one has the inherent supradisciplinarity of ethical discourse within the public domain coupled with a need for professionals to work synergistically with colleagues drawn from other disciplines. Interprofessional ethics is both a key area of cross-disciplinary working practice and a learning device for the enhancement of the mutual understanding and respect needed for successful interdisciplinary teamwork. The maintenance of professional perspectives on moral issues would seem to be an obstacle to effective practice in these areas.

In favour of interdisciplinarity is the fundamental interconnectedness of professional morality and professional role, which suggests that a supradisciplinary ethics alone could not provide the level of support that professionals need if they are to meet the ever-increasing demands of society in matters of conduct and accountability. For example, within healthcare an increasing emphasis on patient-centredness is leading to profound changes in both medicine and nursing. Each profession must define their obligations through a detailed attention to the way their members interact with patients, but the close partnership of doctors and nurses also means that each must take account of the other's response if their working practices are to remain compatible and complementary.

The requirement for professional ethics to maintain a balance between the needs of specific disciplines on the one hand and the demands of interprofessional teamwork on the other lies at the heart of the argument for an ethics of interdisciplinarity. To address this question more fully it may be useful to consider the relationship between professional roles and teamwork in a little more detail.

Single-discipline or intra-disciplinary teams in which a number of individuals perform the same or similar tasks can readily share a professional ethical system, be it discipline-specific or supradisciplinary. Teamwork of this kind is cumulative, in that total output comprises the sum of the outputs of individual workers. Professional codes designed to operate in this context can focus on individual conduct, with each person taking responsibility for their own behaviour, leaving questions as to the moral probity of co-workers to those with managerial or supervisory duties.

Single-discipline teams in which differing but complementary roles are assigned to different team members are not cumulative, in that effective performance by an individual will be a necessary but not a sufficient condition for the team's successful operation. In teamwork of this kind, individuals cannot pursue a successful outcome in isolation and a professional morality that focused solely on individual performance and accountability would not support effective professional practice. Multi- or interdisciplinary teams resemble intradisciplinary teams of this second type in the following respects:

- The team comprises a number of different roles;
- The team functions as a unit in pursuit of the desired outcome(s). Individuals cannot achieve the desired outcome(s) by their own efforts alone;
- The team will only function effectively if the component roles are defined in a complementary way. This means that taken together, these roles must be:
  – Sufficient for the achievement of the desired outcome(s);
  – Compatible: i.e. the conditions for successful performance in one role must not conflict with or undermine the conditions for successful performance of other roles. Where possible, team roles should be mutually supportive.

However, interdisciplinary teams differ from intradisciplinary teams in the following respects:

- Team members have different educational and training histories;
- Team members have no experience (and are not expected to gain experience) of performing other team roles;
- Team members cannot exchange roles with members drawn from different disciplines;

- The professional bodies and codes of practice to which the team members look for guidance can function independently of one another.

The key difference between intra- and interdisciplinary collaboration is that the former allows for a much greater degree of interchangeability between team members. This means that although an individual might perform only a subset of the group's activity, their shared professional identity and background allows them to understand and appreciate the needs, skills, expertise, and functions of the other team members, which in turn facilitates a shared conception of good practice. Interdisciplinary teams, by contrast, have the same compelling need to work synergistically but lack the framework of shared education, training, experience, and knowledge. Education and training that aims to enhance working relationships and develop mutual support mechanisms on the basis of shared professional identity will not answer the needs of those whose working lives are based largely on interprofessional relationships. One cannot approach this problem by recommending that each team member should acquire a facility with the collaborating disciplines since the *raison d'être* of interdisciplinary team work is the pursuit of objectives that require a wider range of knowledge and expertise than can be expected from the members of a single profession or discipline.

The effective allocation of duties within an interprofessional team requires that each participating discipline's role be defined with reference to the expected contributions of the others. For example, it might be deemed essential that someone on a healthcare team should take on the role of patient advocate, representing the views and wishes of the patient when the team meets to make decisions regarding treatment and care. However, a team in which everyone tried to perform this role might be as unsatisfactory as one in which it was fulfilled by no-one, if it resulted in too little attention being paid to the patient's interest in being offered expert advice, or to doubts concerning their competence. Whenever it is the case that a professional role can only be defined effectively by reference to the expected performance of other professions, it seems likely that professional morality will exhibit a similar co-dependency.

An ethics of interdisciplinarity defined on this basis would result in a framework in which:

- Moral obligations are defined in relation to professional role;
- A morally desirable outcome is achievable only if all members of the team behave rightly.

Such a model would need to be designed with care to ensure that it did not undermine the personal responsibility emphasized by professional codes of conduct; it is all too easy for a shared responsibility to become no-one's responsibility. Personal responsibility is more readily retained within a supradisciplinary framework, as team members are asked to step aside from their professional roles when making morally sensitive decisions. However, they can only do this if the following conditions are met:

- Full knowledge: each professional needs access to all information relevant to the moral issue under consideration and the expertise to understand it;
- Impartiality: all interests affected by this issue are relevant to each professional's deliberations and all interest-holders carry equal weight for them;
- Equal responsibility: all team members have an equal responsibility for ensuring the achievement of a morally acceptable outcome;
- Equal authority: each professional's opinion carries equal weight within the moral decision-making arena.

The first of these requirements, the need for full knowledge, is clearly problematic for an interdisciplinary team but is one which is readily overlooked within HE, as students will normally be taught via the consideration of case studies in which all the relevant facts are included. In the workplace, constraints of time and the varying effectiveness of communication channels mean that some team members may be working with a partial set of facts (and in some cases one of the excluded items will be the fact that only a partial set of facts has been presented to them). More fundamentally, moral issues arising from the pursuit of objectives that require input from multiple disciplines may require individuals to consider factors defined in terms that lie outside their own area of expertise. This difficulty could be mitigated by the creation of a permanent learning dimension to interdisciplinary ethics, with team members making every effort to share their knowledge with others, but it will not always be practicable to place all team members on an equal footing. An ethics of interdisciplinarity would therefore need to define a framework in which team members could take colleagues' expert evaluation of morally sensitive facts on trust, even when those facts were primary determinants of the outcome of their moral deliberations.

The notion of impartiality is also subject to some concerns. Interdisciplinary teams often have a duty of service or care to a number of interest-holders but the obligation to serve those interests need not be the same for all team members. For example, some disciplines will give primacy to the interests of their service-user, while others may have an obligation to balance the claims of the service-user against those of third parties, or be concerned with impact on society as a whole. Where professions recognize varying responsibilities with regard to the serving of interests, a moral decision-making framework premised on an assumption of impartiality would undermine the effective performance of individual team roles.

An ethics of interdisciplinarity that allowed for professional role-based variations in knowledge and the serving of interests would require concomitant modifications to moral responsibility, allowing it to follow or "track" performance of professional role. In some cases this might result in each profession having different moral duties but an equal responsibility for the achievement of a morally acceptable outcome. In other circumstances, moral responsibility may be distributed unequally, with the actions of one or two disciplines being of particular moral sensitivity, while other professions have a much smaller contribution to the achievement of a morally acceptable outcome.

Moral authority would vary in a similar way, although it is important to note that this does not mean that it would reflect a profession's usual position in the interprofessional hierarchy (where one exists), for a profession which was subordinate in other respects might be best equipped to take priority moral decision-making. The desirability of maintaining personal accountability for actions would mean that as far as possible, moral authority should go hand-in-hand with moral responsibility, allowing those disciplines which largely determine the achievement of a morally acceptable outcome to have primacy in the moral decision-making process.

An ethics of interdisciplinary defined in these terms would produce a model in which each professional functioned as a co-dependent moral agent, making moral decisions with:

- Professional knowledge: each professional would need access to the information relevant to their role and the expertise to understand it;
- Professional advocacy: each professional would represent the interest-holders with whom their professional duties were mainly concerned;
- Professional responsibility: a professional's obligation to ensure a morally acceptable outcome would be relative to professional role;
- Professional authority: a professional's influence on the outcome of the moral decision-making process would correlate to their level of moral responsibility as defined by professional role.

An ethics of interdisciplinary would then function as a form of professional ethics in which moral decision-making retains a level of discipline-specificity to produce moral roles that parallel professional roles. Individual moral conduct and accountability would be defined in terms of performance of moral roles and would not correlate directly with the achievement of an acceptable moral outcome. Good professional conduct would be a function of the team as a whole, achievable only when all the constituent moral roles were defined correctly and performed successfully.

Conclusion

The primary objective for this discussion has been to suggest what an ethics of interdisciplinarity might be rather than to describe what is. Professional ethics is a rapidly evolving field and although its relationship with interdisciplinarity is of rising importance, there are still more questions than answers concerning the extent to which interdisciplinarity can be accommodated within a broadly supradisciplinary approach.

It has been argued that there are grounds for giving special consideration to the needs of interdisciplinary team-working within the broader context of professional ethics, but more discussion among those actively involved in the development of professional ethics is required, in order to determine whether a framework along the lines outlined above could be made practicable.

Acknowledgment

This chapter was produced as an output of the ETHICS Project, a one year cross-disciplinary initiative funded by the LTSN that aimed to promote examples of effective practice in ethics learning and teaching, drawing on disciplines covered by six subject centres: philosophical and religious studies; bioscience; law; medicine, dentistry and veterinary medicine; psychology and health sciences and practice.

Notes

1. For recent examples see:

   Great Britain Department of Health (2001). *Harold Shipman's clinical practice 1974–1998: A clinical audit commissioned by the Chief Medical Officer.* London: The Stationery Office.

   Royal Liverpool Children's Inquiry—Great Britain Department of Health (2001). *The Report of The Royal Liverpool Children's Inquiry (House of Commons papers 2000–01 12-II).* London: The Stationery Office.

   Bristol Royal Infirmary Inquiry (2001). *The Report of the Public Inquiry into children's heart surgery at the Bristol Royal Infirmary 1984–1995.* London: The Stationery Office.

   BSE Inquiry (2000). *The BSE Inquiry—Inquiry into the emergence and identification of Bovine Spongiform Encephalopathy (BSE) and variant Creutzfeldt-Jakob Disease (vCJD) and the action taken in response to it up to 20 March 1996.* London: The Stationery Office.

   Great Britain Department for Environment, Food and Rural Affairs (2002). *Foot and Mouth Disease: Lessons to be Learned Inquiry Report HC888, (House of Commons papers 2001–02 888).* London: The Stationery Office.

2. To view these resources online see:

   The Home Office's Guide to the use of animals in research on: http://www.homeoffice.gov.uk/comrace/animals/reference.html (last accessed 30/03/04).

   The Wellcome Trust's Biomedical Ethics Program on: http://www.wellcome.ac.uk/en/1/pinbio.html (last accessed 30/03/04).

   The MRC's Centre for Best Practice for Animals in Research on: http://www.mrc.ac.uk/index/public-interest/public-ethics_and_best_practice/public-use_of_animals_in_research/public-cbpar.htm (last accessed 30/03/04).

   The Nuffield Council on: http://www.nuffieldbioethics.org/home/ (last accessed 30/03/04).

   Greenpeace on: http://www.greenpeace.org.uk (last accessed 30/03/04).

The World Wide Fund for Nature on: http://www.wwf.org.uk/ (last accessed 30/03/04).

References

Alderson, P., Farsides, B., and Williams, C. (2002). Examining ethics in practice: health service professionals' evaluations of in hospital ethics seminars. *Nursing Ethics, 9*(5), 508–521.

Beauchamp, T. L., and Childress, J. F. (1994). *Principles of biomedical ethics.* Oxford: Oxford University Press.

Edward, C., and Preece, P. E. (1999). Shared teaching in health care ethics: A report on the beginning of an idea. *Nursing Ethics, 6*(4), 299–307.

LTSN Subject Centre for Health Sciences and Practice (2002). *Interprofessional education: Today, yesterday and tomorrow: A review.* London: LTSN.

Malin, N. A., Wilmot, S., and Beswick, J. A. (2000). The use of an ethical advisory group in a learning disability service. *Journal of Learning Disabilities, 4*(2), 105–114.

Oakley, D., and Cocking, J. (2002). *Virtue ethics and professional roles.* Melbourne: Cambridge University Press.

Peach, L. (Chair) (1999). *Fitness for practice.* Commissioned and published by the United Kingdom Central Council (UKCC) for Nursing, Midwifery and Health Visiting, now the Nursing and Midwifery Council. The Report is viewable online at: http://www.nmc-uk.org/nmc/main/publications/fitnessForPractice.pdf (last accessed 30/03/04).

Robertson, D. W. (1996). Ethical theory, ethnography, and differences between doctors and nurses in approaches to patient care. *Journal of Medical Ethics, 22*(5), 292–299.

Tugcu, P., Hung, R. J., Pan, H. L, Nolan, P. W., and Smith, J. (1995). Ethical awareness among first year medical, dental and nursing students. *International Journal of Nursing Studies, 32*(5), 506–517.

3
Supporting Interdisciplinary Studies Using Learning Technologies

ALLISON LITTLEJOHN

Glasgow Caledonian University

AND

DAVID NICOL

University of Strathclyde

Real-life problems are becoming increasingly complex and depend on knowledge from a variety of different disciplines. This has led to a growth in interdisciplinary and cross-disciplinary or multidisciplinary programs in higher education. In these programs, students in groups are normally expected to solve a problem, often one that is open-ended and complex. This requires that they build a shared understanding of the problem domain while drawing upon a range of information and resources across different disciplinary fields. The intention is to bring together a richness of perspectives and to help students acquire discourses from a variety of disciplines.

E-learning tools can be used to support these processes. For example, some tools (e.g. chat tools and discussion boards) allow students from different disciplines to negotiate and construct a shared understanding of the problem domain without the need to meet face-to-face. Other tools (e.g. shared workspace, e-portfolios) make the sharing of resources easier across members of a group when compared to situations where sharing requires personal contact. This is advantageous in interdisciplinary studies where resources may be quite diverse and drawn from disciplines that may be unfamiliar to some group members.

While the educational principles behind traditional learning are not fundamentally different from the principles underpinning E-learning (Alexander and Boud, 2001) each approach affords different opportunities and constraints. In traditional forms of learning and teaching, interactions are usually face-to-face such as in-class discussions and group-working. E-learning changes the way in which students communicate, access, and share resources, and in what and how they might be assessed. However, an important benefit of campus-based learning is that students have the opportunity to integrate what happens face-to-face with what happens online. This type of "blended learning" makes it possible to combine the best of both traditional and online learning approaches. At the University of South Dakota, blended learning is succinctly defined as "any technologically mediated learning using computers, whether in a face to face classroom setting or from distance learning" (USD, 2004).

In this chapter problem-based learning is used as a pedagogical model to examine how learning technology might support interdisciplinary studies. The chapter starts by considering common misperceptions of E-learning. It then provides a framework for understanding problem-based learning methods and explores ways in which a range of technologies might support problem-based learning. The chapter also discusses issues raised by the use of technology to support learning.

Common Misperceptions about E-learning

Despite the possibilities offered by E-learning, the extra layer of complexity, over and above face-to-face learning, can create problems for tutors who don't plan in advance their use of technology in their teaching. There are three main problem areas.

The first of these arises from confusion over the different ways that technology might support learning. These aspects might be classified as e-administration, e-content delivery, and E-learning. E-administration can be thought of as the use of electronic tools to support access to course information, online registration, and records of achievement. E-delivery is the use of tools that support the management and storage of and access to electronic learning resources. E-learning refers to tools that support learning processes such as the active construction of meaning, reflection, assessment, and feedback (Palinscar and Brown, 1984). While planning E-learning it is important that tutors think through how the technology might support these different aspects of learning and what activities students might need to engage in, in order to learn.

This leads on to a second issue, whether the learning activities should be online or face-to-face. The online–offline balance of activities is influenced by two factors: how easily students can meet (Timms et al., 1999) and the specific learning goals (Ingraham et al., 2002). If students are unable to meet, all interactions must be mediated by communication technologies whereas if they can meet face-to-face such activities can take place in class. There are, however, advantages in using online communication with campus-based learners. For example, asynchronous discussions are recorded and this makes it possible for students to revisit them and to reflect on their past contributions. This would not be possible in a normal face-to-face discussion. Hence if one goal of the learning is to develop writing skills (e.g. making an argument) then asynchronous discussions might play a useful role in the teaching repertoire. Therefore, when planning for E-learning, tutors should take into consideration the location of students, the range of electronic tools that can support learning, and the learning goals of the course.

A third issue concerns the differences between the *nature* of online and face-to-face interactions and the media that support these. The forms of interactions afforded by different media types will vary and one method is likely to be more appropriate to a particular learning situation (Laurillard, 2002, pp. 99–105). Face-to-face discussion and technology-mediated discussion may seem to involve similar discursive processes, but their use can lead to very different outcomes (Nicol et al., 2003). For example, a "bulletin board discussion" may appear similar to a classroom discussion, because both involve some sort of dialog, but there are qualitative differences (Weinberger, 2002). Online discussion is different in its timing, in its structure, and in the discourse conventions used when compared to face-to-face conversation. Online discourse is much more time-consuming on the part of the student and some may prefer the more spontaneous interaction of face-to-face conversations. Therefore, when planning blended learning, tutors should consider a range of tools and choose those that are appropriate to the learning goals (Conole and Fill, 2005).

In summary, when planning E-learning for interdisciplinary studies, it is important that tutors do not merely focus on electronic tools and their affordances. A more effective approach is to use an educational framework to design the teaching and learning and to use tools that support this design. In this chapter problem-based learning is used as a framework for interdisciplinary learning.

Problem-based Learning and Interdisciplinary Studies

Problem-based learning usually begins with an open-ended problem around which students in groups organize their studies. Normally this would involve discussing a problem issue, searching for resources, and working together towards a solution or a set of recommendations. Problem-based learning is appropriate for interdisciplinary studies for two reasons. First, the solution to a problem usually calls for resources from across different disciplinary domains. Second, groups can be set up so that their composition includes students from different disciplines.

The middle column of Table 3.1 depicts the typical stages of problem-based learning. The left-hand column shows where in the problem-based learning process reflective activities occur. These are defined in terms of Cowan's model (1998) where reflection can occur before action, during action, and after action. The purpose of reflection is to raise students' awareness and skills in solving complex problems.

In a study of problem-based learning supported by online technologies Oliver (2001) examined the development of students' critical thinking skills when solving complex problems. He identified three issues that need to be addressed. These issues were directly related to Cowan's (1998) reflective model. First, he found weaknesses in the early stages of problem-based learning

Table 3.1 Stages of problem-based learning

Types of reflection	Stages of problem-based learning	Tools (scenarios)
	1. Complex problem presented (usually based on real life scenario) and students divided into groups	Virtual learning environments tools
Reflection *for* action	2. Problem discussed—students identify what is known, what resources are needed and what strategies to take	Workflow management tools (see scenario 1)
Reflection *in* action	3. Individuals or groups research different issues and gather resources relating to problem	Repository tools (see scenario 2)
Reflection *on* action	4. Resources evaluated in groups in relation to problem	Discussion, email and chat tools (see scenario 3)
	5. Above cycle repeated 3–5 until the problem has been framed adequately and all issues are addressed	
	6. Possible actions, recommendations, solutions generated.	Assignment tool Discussion tools

(reflection for action). Unlike experts in disciplines who spend a lot of time planning when they are faced with a problem, students evinced weaknesses in their initial planning and in workflow management. For example, they often began their investigation of the problem without effective goal-setting and strategy planning. A second issue raised by Oliver was that students place too much emphasis on finding information and resources (content) rather than critically evaluating and interpreting these resources in terms of the problem under investigation (reflection in action). The third issue identified was that students are not good at reflecting back on progress (reflection on action). This may lead to poor evaluation of progress towards the problem's solution. The sections that follow outline how each stage of problem-based learning can be supported with electronic tools as well as how the issues raised by Oliver (2001) might be addressed. While the context used is interdisciplinary studies many of the arguments are relevant to multidisciplinary studies.

Integrated Learning Environment Systems

In recent years, the use of electronic tools has created new opportunities to support interdisciplinary and problem-based learning. These tools are widely available within electronic learning systems such as virtual learning environments, e-portfolios and shared workspaces (Britain and Liber, 2004).

The most commonly used commercial Virtual Learning Environment (VLE) systems are WebCT (www.webct.com) and Blackboard (www.blackboard.com). These systems comprise a collection of integrated tools that enable the management of online learning, that provide a delivery mechanism, student tracking, assessment, and access to resources (Milligan, 1998). These environments support the stages of problem-based learning by:

1. Allowing students to access descriptions of problem tasks, often based on real-life scenarios. Such course or class information can be kept up-to-date through a messaging system or course calendar. (e-administration).
2. Supporting students' reflections on the problem. Students can use asynchronous communications technologies to help them view current resources, to identify what resources are needed, and to decide what strategies to take. Workflow management systems can be created within a VLE to help groups management their time and their document resources (E-learning).
3. Providing a mechanism for individuals or groups to research different issues and gather resources relating to the problem. Resources can be deposited within an electronic repository which may be integral to the VLE. Repository systems provide useful virtual spaces for students working on collaborative group projects. They allow students to upload and share resources and information as mixed media (e-content).
4. Enabling evaluation of these resources by students in groups. This can be achieved through student dialogue using synchronous chat or asynchronous discussions. These tools can also support collaborative learning through shared whiteboards, etc.
5. Hosting students' project assignments. Students can upload final recommendations using assignment drop boxes or email.

Despite the range of VLE systems available, few are being widely used to support problem-based learning (Britain and Liber, 2004). In addition, few tutors specifically link online learning activities and content with face-to-face student interactions (Crook, 2002; Crook and Barrowcliff, 2001). As mentioned earlier, the integration of online and face-to-face is important if students are working on problems within a campus-based environment.

In the scenarios below we propose a number of strategies and online tools that may help to address the issues of problem-based learning in interdisciplinary contexts. Each of the scenarios involves a number of the problem-based learning stages and the tools discussed could support more than one type of reflection (see Table 3.1).

Scenario 1: Workflow Management Tools

A common issue in interdisciplinary learning is managing the project work-flow, documenting progress in terms of problem goals, and making sure that all students share a common understanding of those goals and the sub-goals that define the problem domain. This requires that students record goals, reflect on progress, receive feedback from the tutor and reset goals, plans and strategies based on that feedback, etc. This kind of workflow management is quite difficult to achieve using paper-based systems especially given that students often cannot attend project meetings and access to project resources may be unequal.

One way to overcome this problem is to use workflow management tools. Stefani et al. (2000) report on a project in which students from a variety of disciplines constructed their own goal-setting and planning tool (Figure 3.1) with guidance from their tutor and an educational advisor. The tool comprised folders to store information about the project team and to store digital resources related to the project (generated by students and sourced externally), including a literature review. There were also links to external sites.

A week-by-week progress folder was implemented to encourage reflection. In this problem-based learning scenario the students were required to discuss the project goals, agree gaps in knowledge, and record these goals and areas in need of investigation in the workflow tool (reflection for action). The students also recorded their reflections on what action they would take in the light of comments from their tutors (reflection in action). This comprised the action plan for the coming week.

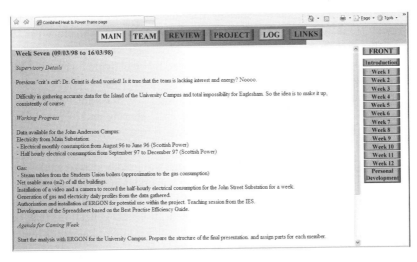

Figure 3.1 Workflow management tool.

This workflow tool supported the whole of the problem-based learning process (reflection in, for and on action) including iterative processes. It was particularly beneficial to problem-based learning in a number of ways. First, the students were able to keep a permanent record of their changing goals and progress. The tool helped make the project goals explicit and helped students in the teams maintain a shared understanding of what these goals were. It was also possible for students to revisit earlier goals and re-examine the problem solving process. Another benefit was that project resources were always available to students even when they were outside the university. This meant that anyone in the team could update files at a time convenient to them. From the teacher's perspective, these weekly activities made it easy to identify students in particular difficulty and to take action to facilitate their progress. Finally, both students and staff were able to monitor team progress.

Scenario 2: Resource Repositories and Shared Workspaces

A second important aspect of interdisciplinary learning is the evaluation of learning resources in terms of the problem under investigation. Stages two to four of problem-based learning require students to define the problem domain and identify gaps. Strategies to address these gaps include sourcing materials useful to the project and reflecting upon the relevance of these resources in relation to the problem domain (reflection in action). In practice, however, students tend to focus on *finding* content materials, rather than on evaluating their significance relative to the problem in hand (Nicol et al., 2005). Evaluation of materials can be particularly difficult in interdisciplinary studies where students come from different areas of study and where the resources required to solve a problem derive from different disciplines. The evaluation process can be aided by tools that allow resources to be shared and viewed from a central location. One such tool is a digital repository. A digital repository can be viewed as a store of electronic resources collected together at a variety of levels: national, institutional, departmental, small group, or individual (Duncan and Ekmekcioglu, 2003).

In a recent study, Nicol et al. (2005) showed two ways in which digital repositories might be used to support students' sharing and evaluation of resources. First, a repository or shared workspace (the latter refers to an active repository with a range of tools for shared learning as opposed to a repository used merely to deposit and catalogue resources) was used by design students to store and share resources related to a design issue under investigation. Some of these resources were generated by students themselves while carrying out the project while others were sourced externally from formal collections (e.g. the Resource Discovery Network http://www.rdn.ac.uk/) and uploaded or hyper-linked into the shared workspace. The value to students of this central access point for resources was that those within project teams could find information

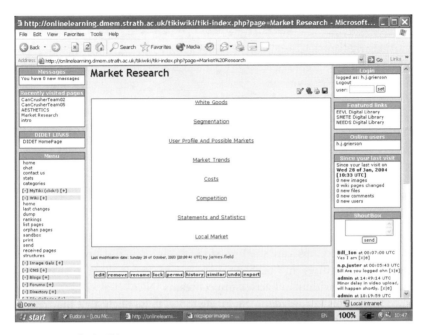

Figure 3.2 Linked wiki pages.

relatively easily. This is particularly useful within this interdisciplinary project where resources derived from a variety of sources.

The second way in which the repository supported learning was by providing tools that enabled students to collaborate in the building of a shared representation of the problem or issue under investigation. During their problem-based learning, students were asked to create knowledge structures that illustrated their conceptual thinking about the design problem and to communicate this to others outside their team. This was achieved in two ways (Grierson et al., 2004). In one study, the students constructed a set of inter-linked wiki pages (like web pages) using a tool in the shared workspace (Figure 3.2). These interlinked pages illustrated the team's shared understanding about how they interpreted the resources they had studied during the group project. In another study, the students collaboratively constructed a "concept map" using a tool within the shared workspace (Figure 3.3). Both these tools enabled students to provide a visual representation of the problem domain that could be shared. Moreover, the nodes of the concept map could be linked directly to the relevant resources, providing a way of linking knowledge structures to resource structures.

It is important that students have opportunities to organize their interpretation of resources in personal ways that suit group members and their ways

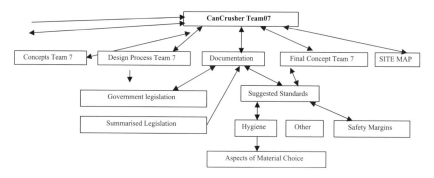

Figure 3.3 Concept map with nodes hyperlinked to related resources.

of working (Nesbit and Winne, 2003). These tools within digital repositories or shared workspaces can support students as they collaboratively create knowledge structures in a problem domain and enable them to share these representations within and across project teams (Nicol et al., 2005). We have called these tools "knowledge-structuring tools" to highlight that they refer to the organization of concepts, ideas, facts, and formulae in ways that would represent the groups' understanding of the problem domain. This is different from tools that help students to structure resources (e.g. in hierarchies of folders and sub-folders).

Knowledge-structuring is important for problem-based learning because the more opportunities students have to actively interrelate concepts, ideas, facts, and rules with each other and with prior knowledge, the deeper the understanding and learning (Jonassen and Carr, 2000). There is also consensus amongst researchers that one characteristic of experts in any professional domain is that they possess well-organized and flexibly accessible internal knowledge structures (DeCorte, 1988). In addition, for effective learning, it is student-generated knowledge structures that are important, not structures provided by tutors (Jonassen et al., 1993).

Scenario 3: Discussion Tools

Another issue in problem-based learning is that students working in a group may have different views of the problem and different understandings of the goals. This issue is particularly problematic within the context of interdisciplinary learning where discourses across disciplines are different and misunderstandings about the meaning of terms are more likely. The online environment can provide tools to help address this issue.

One example is the use of a web page editing tool to support the collaborative construction of online posters (Morris and Pilkington, 2004). In a "Land Management" course at the University of Sussex, where students were enrolled from a variety of subject disciplines, tutors identified problems with the meaning assigned to concepts and technical terms within the interdisciplinary groups. They therefore devised a problem-based activity to support students in becoming familiar with these terminologies and developing a shared understanding.

Students, working in small, interdisciplinary teams, were required to collaboratively construct e-posters describing one aspect of land management. Each e-poster was a web page constructed and edited by the group. This task involved students collaboratively planning, constructing the poster, and reflecting back on its impact. These activities encouraged reflection and helped students gain insight into different perspectives and discourses across disciplines and led to improved understanding of concepts and terms.

Another way to address misunderstandings within groups is to make available asynchronous bulletin boards so that students can discuss and share ideas and develop shared understandings. Bulletin boards are available in almost all VLEs. In a recent unpublished study students used a bulletin board to help them understand terms they were unsure of. In the past tutors provided glossaries or definitions of terms but this proved unsuccessful. Some definitions were still not understood by team members and the tutors were not able to provide glossaries for every term that might arise during an open-ended problem.

The bulletin board was used to address this by supporting students in the construction of their own glossary of terms. The students worked in groups and each group managed its own "translation board" with students "translating" formal terminology by providing a definition. They then shared their definitions across a number of groups and discussed which solution was best. An advantage of such created glossaries is that they provide a reusable resource that can be used by subsequent cohorts of students. However, there are merits in students constructing their own "translation boards" and comparing their ideas against exemplars from other student groups rather than being given a dictionary list produced by a previous cohort of students. This can help students with reflection *for* action.

In both these examples a variety of other asynchronous communication tools might have been used; tools such as "blogs" or "wikis" (web pages that can be edited by multiple users) may have been equally effective. All these tools help support reflection—during planning (for action), while gathering and discussing resources (in action), and when evaluating progress (on action).

These tools offer some advantages over face-to-face discussion. Online asynchronous discussion is written rather than spoken. Hence a permanent record of the discussion is available. This means students can reflect upon past discussions and learn from them. For example, if the discussion led to the solution to a problem the students would be able to review the record of the problem-solving process.

Lesson Plans to Support Interdisciplinary E-learning

To make the best use of E-learning tools it is necessary to formulate a *lesson plan* (Littlejohn et al., 2003). Lesson plans can help tutors address the three problem areas associated with planning E-learning outlined at the beginning of this chapter. First, by focusing on the design of student learning activities, problems caused by the confusion of E-learning practice with e-administration and e-content delivery processes can be reduced. This approach ensures that learner interaction is central to design considerations. Second, by mapping tutor and student activities against online and offline environments, the integration of online and face-to-face activities can be strengthened. This approach also allows consideration of how feedback would be offered to students. Third, the lesson plan can help in the selection of appropriate methods of communication and media forms. This is achieved by mapping online and offline activities against relevant e-tools.

Lesson plans can be structured as matrices that map learning activities against core elements of teaching, learning, and assessment: tutor roles, student roles, content resources, service resources, and feedback (Nicol and Littlejohn, 2005). This form of matrix structure is, potentially, a useful tool for planning E-learning for campus-based students, since it can be used to map the integration of online and face-to-face activities. An example of a lesson plan for the "translation board" activity in scenario three is illustrated in Table 3.2.

This lesson plan illustrates the integration of students' face-to-face and online interactions while constructing the translation board. It documents new content resources generated as outputs from the learning activities, including, in this case, glossaries of terms written in language that is accessible to the students. The lesson plan itself is a resource that could be reused by the tutor across a range of educational settings and the core elements could be altered to fit any new context (Conole and Fill, 2005; Laurillard and McAndrew, 2003). Its structure allows the tutor to appraise and adjust the strategy for assessment and feedback. This is particularly helpful for tutors when they are thinking through the ways in which students will use electronic tools to support their reflection for, on, and in action.

The Future of E-learning and Interdisciplinary Education

Collaborative, problem-based learning is a good way of realizing the potential of interdisciplinary and multidisciplinary studies. It allows students to engage in real-life problems in ways that help them to integrate knowledge from a variety of domains. Online environments and tools can enhance learning in interdisciplinary and multidisciplinary contexts. They can be used to support all stages of problem-based learning. They allow tutors to administer courses and disseminate learning resources. They support the building of

Table 3.2 A lesson plan of scenario 3

	Tutor role	Student role	Resources (Content)	Resources (Services)	Assessment/Feedback
Face-to-face	Divide students into groups; Introduce students to task				
Online	Initiate a "translation" list on a separate board. Place some words and translations as exemplars (online); Moderate stage 1 discussion (online)	Each student group investigates one piece of evidence for evolution; Students upload terms they are unsure about into a "translation" board—then respond to others by providing definitions in their own words.	"Evolution and Early Development" article (.doc)	Discussion Board for translation	Formative assessment: the meanings of terms; Peer feedback on meanings of terms; Tutor feedback when terminology is misunderstood.
Face-to-face	Give feedback re translations and encourage continued use	Group discussions offline (in class) about evidence. Group agrees on a summary and group summary writer posts this to the discussion board.	Translations created by students	Discussion board	Feedback from peers during group discussion
Online	Monitor boards, ask relevant questions to stimulate discussion	Post initial group summary; Read postings from other groups.	Translations created by student groups	Discussion board	Feedback from student groups to other groups. Overview from tutor—summary of main issues articulated by student groups.
Face-to-face	Monitor discussion boards	Determine what the common themes are across groups (by accessing bulletin boards and holding face-to-face group discussions)—Post ideas to submission board.			Formative assessment: determining common themes. Feedback from other students and tutor.

Source: Used with kind permission from Jane Tobias, Bell College, Hamilton, U.K.

a shared understanding of the project goals by students. They provide tools to facilitate the sourcing, storage, and integration of resources from different disciplinary domains. However, it is important that the use of electronic tools is driven by educational considerations rather than by technological considerations.

Over the next five to ten years, E-learning tools and processes will become increasingly integrated. Students are already using their own mobile phones to discuss ideas, search for internet resources, and create digital, still, and moving images. Improved interoperability across digital repositories, workflow management tools, shared workspaces, and discussion tools will further support student reflection during collaborative, problem-based learning.

However, to maximize interdisciplinary learning we need to recognize that incoming students think and work in different ways from their tutors and that they are more sophisticated in their use of technologies than their tutors. In the future we may need to draw on the expertise of our students when designing effective, technology-supported, interdisciplinary courses.

References

Alexander, S., and Boud, D. (2001). Learners still learn from experience when online. In J. Stephenson (Ed.), *Teaching and learning online* (pp. 3–15). Kogan Page: London.

Britain, S., and Liber, O. (2004). *A framework for pedagogical evaluation of virtual learning environments.* JISC commissioned report.

Conole, G., and Fill, K. (2005). A learning design toolkit to create pedagogically effective learning activities. *Journal of Interactive Media in Education, 08*, 1–16.

Cowan, J. (1998), *On becoming an innovative university teacher: Reflection in action.* London: SRHE and Open University Press.

Crook, C. K. (2002). The campus experience of networked learning. In C. Steeples and C. Jones (Eds.), *Networked learning: Issues and perspectives* (pp. 293–308). Springer: London.

Crook, C. K., and Barrowcliff, D. (2001). Ubiquitous computing on campus: Patterns of engagement by university students. *International Journal of Human–computer Interaction, 13*(2), 245–258.

DeCorte, E. (1988) New perspectives on learning and teaching in higher education. In A. Burgen (Ed.), *Goals and purposes of higher education in the twenty-first century.* London: Jessica Kingsley Publishers.

Duncan, C., and Ekmekcioglu, C. (2003). Digital libraries and repositories. In A. H. Littlejohn (Ed.), *Reusing online resources* (pp. 135–145). London: Kogan Page.

Grierson, H., Nicol, D., Littlejohn, A., and Wodehouse, A. (2004) Structuring and sharing information resources to support concept development and design learning. Network Learning Conference April 5–7, 2004, Lancaster, United Kingdom.

Ingraham, B., Watson, B., McDowell, L., Brockett, A., and Fitzpatrick, S. (2002). Evaluating and implementing learning environments: A United Kingdom experience. *Educational Technology Review, 10*(2). http://www.aace.org/pubs/etr/issue3/ingraham.cfm.

Jonassen, D. H., and Carr, C. (2000). Mindtools: Affording multiple knowledge representations in learning. In S. P. Lajoie (Ed.), *Computers as cognitive tools, Vol. 2: No more walls* (pp. 165–196). Mahwah, NJ: Lawrence Erlbaum Associates.

Jonassen, D. H., Beissner, K., and Yacci, M. (1993). *Structural knowledge: Techniques for representing, conveying and acquiring structural knowledge.* Hillsdale, NJ: Lawrence Erlbaum Associates.

Laurillard, D. (2002). *Rethinking university teaching* (2nd ed.). London: RoutledgeFalmer.

Laurillard, D., and McAndrew, P. (2003). Reusable educational software: A basis for generic learning activities. In A. Littlejohn (Ed.), *Reusing online resources: A sustainable approach to E-learning* (pp. 81–93). London: Kogan Page.

Littlejohn, A., Jung, I., and Broumley, L. (2003). A comparison of issues in the reuse of resources in schools, colleges and universities. In A. Littlejohn (Ed.), *Reusing online resources: A sustainable approach to E-learning* (pp. 212–220). London: Kogan Page.

Milligan, C. (1998). The role of virtual learning environments in the online delivery of staff development. http://www.jisc.ac.uk/uploaded_documents/jtap-044.doc.

Morris, J., and Pilkington, M. (2004). Using WebCT to enhance learning for part-time students. University of Sussex Teaching and Learning Conference, November 2004.

Nesbit, J. C., and Winne, P. H. (2003). Self-regulated inquiry with networked resources. *Canadian Journal of Learning and Technology, 29*(3). http://www.cjlt.ca/content/vol29.3/cjlt29-3_art5.html.

Nicol, D., and Littlejohn, A. (2005). Designing E-learning: Developing effective lesson plans. University of Strathclyde, unpublished manuscript.

Nicol, D., Littlejohn, A., and Grierson, H. (2005). The importance of structuring information and resources within shared workspaces during collaborative design learning. *Open Learning, 2*(1), 31–49.

Nicol, D., Minty, I., and Sinclair, C. (2003) The social dimensions of online learning. *Innovations in Education and Training International, 40*(3), 270–280.

Oliver, R. (2001). Exploring the development of critical thinking skills through a web-supported problem-based learning environment. In J. Stephenson (Ed.), *Teaching and learning online* (pp. 98–111). London: Kogan Page.

Palinscar, A. S., and Brown, A. L. (1984). Reciprocal teaching of comprehension-fostering and comprehension-monitoring activities. *Cognition and Instruction, 1*(2), 117–175.

Stefani, L. A. J., Clarke, J., and Littlejohn, A. H. (2000). Developing a student centred approach to reflecting on learning innovations. *Education and Training International, 37*(2), 163–171.

Timms, D., Booth, S., Crompton, P., Klein, B., Bangali, L., and Schnuekel, B. (1999). Review of telematics based open and distance learning, *European Commission Educational Multimedia Taskforce Schema*. http://www.schema.stir.ac.uk/Deliverables/D6.1.pdf.

USD (2004). *University of South Dakota Glossary of Library and Internet Terms*. http://www.usd.edu/library/instruction/glossary.shtml.

Weinberger, D. (2002) *Small pieces loosely joined*. Cambridge, MA: Perseus Publishing.

4

Assessment in Interdisciplinary and Interprofessional Programs
Shifting Paradigms

LORRAINE STEFANI

University of Auckland

Introduction

The principles of good assessment of student learning in interdisciplinary and interprofessional programs are the same that apply in any other type of program. It is incumbent upon course and program designers to use models of curriculum development which seek to align the assessment strategy with the intended or stated learning outcomes of any course (Biggs, 2003; Cowan and Harding 1986; Miller et al., 1998). There is, however, significant anecdotal evidence to indicate that many programs of study have evolved over a period of time rather than having been designed on the basis of a pedagogically underpinned model of curriculum development (Stefani, 2004). Within higher education there has long been the tradition that any assessment strategy must be above all valid, reliable (e.g. Ramsden, 1992, 2003), and appropriate irrespective of the fact that reliable assessment and appropriate assessment may in essence sometimes be attributes in conflict. As will be highlighted in this chapter, this may well be the situation for some interdisciplinary programs of study.

As our understanding of the dynamics and the complexity of teaching and learning increases (Prosser and Trigwell, 1999) so too does our level of unease regarding the assessment of student learning. An assessment method is valid if it actually assesses that which it is designed to assess, and a reliable assessment tool/instrument/strategy is viewed as one which produces consistent results (Ramsden, 2003; TEDI, 2001). However, as Elton (2003) has pointed out, for too long assessment strategies have been dominated by the demand for reliability above everything else. Elton argues that the primary reason for this inappropriate use of the reliability factor has been "that all the individual assessments within a degree course had in the end to be correlated into a single number—the degree class." Elton argues that to correlate assessments of different reliabilities in this manner is inappropriate. His view is that learning outcomes which cannot be assessed with a high degree of reliability have been hugely undervalued. Examples of work which are generally undervalued include practical work, group projects, and in some cases work placements. Such an argument may be of great importance in relation to interdisciplinary and interprofessional programs wherein there is great scope for "authentic" assessment.

"Authentic assessment" is becoming a more desirable means of judging student ability because it entails setting learning tasks as closely related as possible to those that would be involved in the profession to which the degree is orientated (TEDI, 2001; Wiggins, 1993). An example of this might be a student working with a real patient on the management of designing and fitting a prosthesis. Non-authentic assessment would be based on a text-book treatise on prosthesis fitting. The authenticity here lies in the fact that a "real patient" requires a well-fitted prosthesis—but the "reliability factor" fails because an entire class of students cannot work with one patient—and all patients will require different fittings and possibly different management of that fitting. "Case-based" assessment is another example of authentic assessment which is particularly suited to interdisciplinary and interprofessional courses—based on the understanding that the whole point of interdisciplinary courses is the potential to find novel solutions to complex problems (Silverman and Welty, 1996).

For example, it may be that a case-based scenario such as developing a sustainable public transport system for the Auckland region requires a multidisciplinary or interdisciplinary approach and that there are a number of novel potential "solutions" to this problem. The case study is a valid learning task, but how can reliability be built into the assessment strategy?

The issues of the lack of coherent curriculum design and of the reliability factor in assessment of student learning have potentially presented barriers to the satisfactory development of a wider range of interdisciplinary courses than is currently available to students entering into higher education. A further barrier is the reality of "academic tribes and territories" (Becher, 1989; Becher and Trow, 2001), where the primary allegiance of academic staff is to their disciplinary base. Academic staff become "encultured" into the language and traditions of their discipline. They in turn, possibly sub-consciously, "enculture" their students into that discipline (Godfrey, 2003; Lave and Wenger, 1991). Any "perceived" dilution of a disciplinary culture will be strongly resisted by academic staff. However, in a changing world, where knowledge is transient (Breivik, 1998) and the ability to transform and manipulate knowledge to solve more complex problems is a key to economic success and sustainability, there is surely a need to overcome these barriers and allow interdisciplinarity and interprofessionalism to flourish.

The remainder of this chapter will explore a number of these issues in greater detail, relating to: the concept of interdisciplinary and interprofessional courses; some current models of interdisciplinarity; the concept of developing the curriculum for interdisciplinary/interprofessional courses; and some suggestions for effective assessment strategies.

The Growth in Potential for Interdisciplinarity/Interprofessionalism

Several factors have combined to create the need for higher education to undergo a rigorous review of itself and reconsider its overall purpose (Henkel, 2000). For almost two decades the notion that higher education is an incontestably good thing which serendipitously meets the economic as well as the social and cultural needs of society has been continuously challenged (Boys et al., 1988). In the lifespan of academia, this is a very short space of time, yet the changes in the concept of higher education have been dramatic. Government policies, particularly but certainly not exclusively within the U.K., have been promoting more explicit relationships between higher education and the labour market (NCIHE, 1997, known as the Dearing Report). Pressure has been brought to bear on universities to redefine the "transmission of academic knowledge" in terms of developing a range of "transferable disciplinary specific and learning skills" in addition to "absorbing disciplinary based knowledge" (Kember, 1997). In tandem with the transferable skills movement, there has been a rapid shift from an elitist system, to one of mass higher education.

Students are now entering into university with a variety of different qualifications; the widening of access policies aimed at attracting students from "non-traditional" backgrounds means pressure for choice of subjects open to this new, diverse student population (Ainley, 1994; Longworth, 1999). Other issues have also pushed the need for different types of courses available to students. During the late 1980s and through the 1990s there was growing concern regarding a "national crisis," especially in the U.K., regarding levels of "mathematical ability" (Tariq, 2002).

This posed major problems for some subject areas. Engineering departments for example began to diversify from "heavy" engineering subjects to "softer" areas such as environmental engineering (Godfrey, 2003), which often required less rigorous mathematical input. Within the sciences, the expansion and growth in biomedical fields of study has made the boundaries between different disciplines more fluid, creating more potential for interdisciplinary courses and programs.

In the early 1990s, within the U.K. but also in other countries such as Australia, there was a dramatic shift in the way that medicine is taught. This came about partly due to the expansion in number of students, but was also due to other factors. Firstly there was a strong perception of a curriculum which could grow uncontrollably in content terms but which in some way failed to embed the concept of skills development, particularly in the area of communication skills (Heylings and Stefani, 1997). Another factor was the change in the way that medical care is delivered and this opened the way for more scope regarding interprofessional courses.

With such a range of factors militating for the development of inter-disciplinary/interprofessional courses, it raises the question of how academics conceive of such programs. The next section explores this issue.

Conceptions of Interdisciplinary/Interprofessional Programs of Study

As mentioned above, academics have a strength of allegiance to their own dis-cipline (Becher and Trow, 2001) which can pose a barrier to the development of innovative programs of study. In researching material for this chapter, how-ever, it became apparent that many staff are not necessarily clear about what "interdisciplinary" actually means. Some staff consider that "interdisciplinary teaching and learning" means teaching and learning which crosses traditional disciplinary boundaries and that this term applies to longstanding areas of study such as "education" for example. Another conception is that the term "interdisciplinary" may be more associated with new areas of enquiry such as "cultural studies," "development studies," etc.

From an educational developer's viewpoint, one of the complications of "interdisciplinary subjects" is that the instructors may be more rooted in one discipline than another. An interdisciplinary program needs a teaching team with broad disciplinary origins. This teaching team then needs to work together to develop a concept of shared territory, and to reach shared concep-tions of the curriculum for interdisciplinary programs (B. M. Grant, personal communication, 2004).

There can be a further complication regarding interdisciplinary programs of study, relating to student learning and to the potential for a research culture. Students may not receive an effective "enculturation" into the means/methodologies/basic principles of any of the "parent" disciplines and it may be difficult for staff who are deeply entrenched within a particular discipline to develop alternative research paradigms and epistemologies suited to a new and different subject area.

Before we can think of effective assessment strategies, we must consider how best to conceptualize "interdisciplinarity." In essence, many disciplines contain within them a range of subject areas or sub-disciplines. If there is a positive agreement to develop an interdisciplinary program, and staff from different disciplines and sub-disciplines come together to design the program, this would be considered to be a multidisciplinary group. If this group then com-mits to considering how complex issues could be interpreted using the skills and methodologies deriving from their various disciplinary areas, this becomes an interdisciplinary project/program. Taking this a step further, the know-ledge and understandings which can derive from this approach become transdisciplinary knowledge (i.e. transformation of knowledge) (Richard le Heron, personal communication, 2005). Viewed in this way, it is clear that the potential for interdisciplinary, or transdisciplinary programs of study is enormous, provided we can move beyond the hindrance of academic politics.

However, for this to happen in a meaningful way it is important that careful attention is paid to the design, development, and delivery of the interdisciplinary/transdisciplinary curriculum, including the assessment strategy. The next section explores some current models of interdisciplinary and interprofessional courses and interrogates the ways in which effective assessment has been considered in these contexts.

The Interdisciplinary Curriculum

Despite the overwhelming changes in the culture and mission of higher education and the increasing interest in the quality of learning and teaching (HEA, 2006; NCIHE, 1997) it is, in this author's experience, the exception rather than the rule that institutional recruitment practices question applicants for academic posts on their learning and teaching philosophy. There is, however, a growing trend towards enhancement of teaching and learning in HE through encouraging staff new to lecturing to complete postgraduate programs relating specifically to academic practice (HEA, 2006).

To support staff in developing new and challenging programs of study we must pose the questions: what is understood by "the curriculum"? How is it designed, developed, and delivered? What factors do curriculum developers and course designers need to take into consideration especially in the design of interdisciplinary/interprofessional programs?

At the University of Auckland, the Tertiary Fine Arts School, ELAM, prides itself on "a strong interdisciplinary approach to Fine Arts Teaching." The school is structured as a series of seven interlinking sections (Painting, Sculpture, Printmaking, Photography, Intermedia Design, and Te Hoi Hou or Maori Arts). The way in which interdisciplinarity is understood in this context is that:

1. First year teaching comprises a series of projects each based primarily in a *single medium* but which allow for students to view media together or to stray across media when responding to a project brief.

2. From the second year of study, Level II, students enter into one of the seven sections listed above. They are taught by staff with expertise mainly in one discipline and the teaching concentrates on that discipline. However, many students in the Painting section (for example) do not make paintings exclusively or sometimes do not make paintings at all. This is normal and is even encouraged. There is no specifically "interdisciplinary" teaching/facilitation of student learning for these non-painting students. Rather, they generally work in an autonomous independent manner, and as necessary liaise with a staff member who specializes in another discipline. This situation has never been addressed in a pedagogical manner, but, based on the key quality

assurance indicators, students working in this way generally perform very well (Nuala Gregory, personal communication 2004).

With respect to assessment of student work, there is no requirement for students to do anything that is particularly "interdisciplinary." Students are assessed on how well they have understood the theme/text/concept they have chosen to respond to and on the quality of the art work produced in response.

A key interdisciplinary aspect of the teaching and learning is in "group teaching," the fact that a mixed group of students from different fine arts disciplines can be brought together in a structured way. No specialist knowledge of the different disciplines is required to carry out the teaching in this context, but a good knowledge of different disciplines is required to facilitate the student learning. Tutors assessing across disciplines must have sufficient knowledge of each separate discipline to be able to assess what is contemporary and imaginative as opposed to what is stale and derivative and which art works show good technique. This is reflected in the criteria used to judge student attainment, which are as follows: conceptual and inventive abilities, ability to research and process information, resolution and presentation of work, studio and professional practice, and overall quality of work.

This means of facilitating student learning has evolved over a period of time and has been "successful" in terms of standard quality indicators. However, the student population is changing and student expectations are changing as a consequence. What ELAM staff are now recognizing, as a direct consequence of teaching quality enhancement procedures within the institution, is that the curriculum needs to be reconceptualized on the basis of current pedagogical models and that the assessment criteria need to be expressed differently to raise awareness, within a changing student population, of what is considered to be meritorious. In other words there is a recognition that the assessment criteria are not sufficiently transparent to necessarily be understood by the students in the way the staff intended them to be understood (Peter Shand, University of Auckland, personal communication, 2005).

This is an example of aspiring to true interdisciplinarity but there is a clear recognition that the curriculum has evolved in this way, rather than having been coherently designed. A curriculum development project with ELAM staff working in partnership with staff from the educational development unit is currently underway to address the issues outlined. This project was initiated by academic staff in ELAM and negotiated with staff from the educational development unit. What is essential in the case of partnership projects of this nature is that the academic staff within the discipline are given the encouragement and scope to have their ideas inbuilt into the proposed curriculum and feel a sense of ownership over the process of program development. Within a school of art, special consideration must be given to the issue of creativity and hence the importance of the learning process when assessment criteria are considered (Hammond and Stefani, 2001).

Another example of the creation of "interdisciplinarity" is where for reasons of expedience different departments/disciplinary bases are conjoined. This situation is not always immediately conducive to the development of truly interdisciplinary programs of study. An example of this applied to the School of Geography and Environmental Science at the University of Auckland. As the title of the school suggests, it was created from the Departments of Geography and Environmental Science on the grounds that there was too much overlap in the study programs being offered by the individual departments.

While this school was created in 2001, there was an inevitable period of time when the changed circumstance existed in name only. Perhaps, not surprisingly, territorial, historical, and cultural issues provided barriers to the design and delivery of truly interdisciplinary curricula. This may be surprising given the outcomes of the research by Becher (1989) which tended to indicate that geography may be a discipline in which its practitioners readily absorb ideas, techniques, and methodologies from neighboring intellectual territories. It may be, therefore, that the process by which the departments were joined focussed initially more on administrative issues than on pedagogical considerations to bring staff together to discuss curriculum development. However, the school has fully recognized and appreciated that in terms of how it is viewed by potential students and potential funders for research projects, it needs to constantly review and update what it offers and how best to exploit the skill sets which exist within. The staffing of the school comprises environmental sciences, itself a subject area which has at its core areas of the biological sciences such as ecology, human geography, political economy, physical geography, and spatial analysis, and geography which also encompasses a range of sub-disciplinary subject areas. The research and scholarship potential is vast and it took time and effort for the staff to recognize and respect each other's intellectual boundaries and accommodate these within an overall ethos of unity.

A professional development project undertaken within the School, again in partnership with the educational development unit, was the review of its scholarly position. To achieve this meant a series of strategic vision/strategic planning sessions to explore the educational purpose and mission of the school: the potential for truly interdisciplinary research projects and the nature of programs of study which can be offered using the range of knowledge, skills, and expertise existing within the staff. Once again this is a project initiated by staff within the school and negotiated with staff from the Professional Development Centre.

Follow-up to the strategic vision sessions included curriculum design and development workshops facilitated within the school. These provided a perfect opportunity to design, develop, and deliver interdisciplinary programs of study, wherein the assessment strategies are now considered in alignment with the intended learning outcomes (Biggs, 2003). We should not underestimate the importance of facilitating development work of this nature in such a way that all staff who will be responsible for delivering and assessing courses and programs feel included in the process.

One example of an entire faculty working together to develop a coherent "interdisciplinary" education for its students comes from the Faculty of Health Sciences at the University of Sydney (Everingham, 2001; Harris and Viney, 2003). To address the challenges in meeting its commitment to the provision of high-quality programs which have currency both educationally and within the employment market, and the challenge associated with sweeping changes to the health service delivery system and the processes associated with providing clinical services, the faculty staff worked together through a series of proposals to develop a vision for the development of interdisciplinary and interprofessional programs.

To move forward with this a whole-of-faculty approach was taken with extensive rounds of meetings, discussions and consultations, and workshops facilitated to develop the themes conducive to a concept of a curricular framework for each undergraduate course provided by the faculty.

These ten themes are as follows:

- Appropriate knowledge systems;
- Inquiry- and evidence-based curricula;
- Multi-professional, multidisciplinary environment;
- Work-focussed curricula;
- Flexible learning;
- First year student experience;
- Assessment for learning and performance;
- Adult learning;
- Learning generic skills;
- Living in an ever-changing workplace.

In expressing these ten themes, there was an acknowledgement that many of them were currently considered within the faculty but that there might need to be a shift in the balance of their emphasis within curricula and in faculty practices.

Shifts in practices would include:

- An increased whole-of-faculty perspective;
- A more multi-professional, multidisciplinary learning environment;
- More collaborative teaching;
- Greater co-ordination of curricular review and change;
- More alliances across faculties, institutions, and professions;
- Responsibility for the profession increasingly shared with students;

- Greater use of flexible approaches to learning and learning pathways (Harris and Viney, 2003).

The above "shifts" in practice represent a strenuous agenda to be followed to develop the types of course and to support the quality of graduate to which this faculty aspires. However, what the agenda indicates is a structured, coherent way forward to manage the changes deemed necessary to respond to changing social and pedagogical demands.

This agenda does not touch on the finer details of the model of curriculum development which will be used to inform the precise components of the learning, teaching, and assessment agenda. Clearly, therefore, even within this highly successful faculty in which the academic staff are working in interrelated fields of the health sciences, it is necessary for all staff to take ownership of the "changed agenda" if the successful design development and delivery of interdisciplinary/interprofessional courses is to be successfully effected.

While there is a movement, particularly in the U.S., to think of a curriculum less as a sequence of independent courses and more as a set of highly integrated learning and assessment experiences designed to help students develop clearly defined outcomes, the will must be there in the first place to achieve this but also the curriculum development knowledge and understanding must be there to underpin this movement.

Daniel Shapiro describes the development of an interdisciplinary program at California State University. At this university the Department of Earth Systems Science and Policy brought together staff from chemistry, physics, biology, geology, ecology, economics, environmental ethics, and teacher education to create an Environmental Science and Policy degree program designed to provide students with the interdisciplinary, critical thinking and technical skills necessary to develop workable solutions to complex environmental problems (Shapiro, 2003).

Shapiro describes a situation where he himself is employed in the institution as an educational developer with the remit to work across faculties to facilitate the development of interdisciplinary curricula. Where the "interdisciplinary" issue is of prime importance is in the development of what are called "capstone programs." This program is undertaken by senior students who work on a "capstone project" for at least two semesters and then present a thesis for assessment. The overall point of the capstone project is to engender critical thinking, taking an interdisciplinary approach to problem-solving.

In a previous publication Shapiro (2002) relates the development of a capstone assessment tool that explicitly links the capstone project to the rest of the curriculum through the overall learning outcomes. In this system, there is a core learning outcome, presumably with associated criteria and the students can/must then choose two further learning outcomes from a list of eleven outcomes which best fit with their project.

There are potential parallels between the way that Harris and her team (2003) are conceptualizing an interdisciplinary/interprofessional curriculum in the health sciences and Shapiro's description of the development of interdisciplinary capstone projects. What is intriguing from Shapiro's work is the idea of providing students with a choice of learning outcomes to suit their project. This is a model which may be ideally translated into other interdisciplinary areas of study where a major concept is the transformation of knowledge by applying multidisciplinary knowledge, skills, and research methodologies to new and complex problems.

Shifting Paradigms: Assessment in an Interdisciplinary Context

In most degree courses and pathways there is a range of assessment tasks according to the discipline, modes of facilitation of learning, expected standards of achievement, and requirements of professional bodies.

This range of assessment tasks may be expected to include:

- essays, reports, problem-solving exercises, case studies;
- laboratory-based practical or creative work;
- group-based projects;
- field work;
- computer-based tests;
- on-line discussions;
- clinical assessment;
- portfolios of evidence;
- dissertations or projects.

This list is not exhaustive, but the important aspects of any form of assessment are the criteria on which the learning outcomes of the program are based.

With respect to interdisciplinary programs, the overall assessment strategy will depend on the model upon which interdisciplinarity is based. For example, according to Knight and Yorke (2003), in modular programs whereby students can choose which units of study to pursue, their development in subject disciplines may be less structured than in single-subject programs. A lack of immersion in a single subject might mean that multidisciplinary students would not do as well in that area as their mono disciplinary peers (Knight and Yorke, 2003). However, this may be more dependent on restrictions on choice of subjects or prerequisites for pursuing particular units of study.

Many subject areas—or multi-subject areas of study such as medicine and engineering—are turning to a problem-based learning (PBL) paradigm as a suitable mode of study. This learning mode involves a different approach to teaching and more innovative approaches to assessment of learning. Much PBL involves students working in groups, a situation which enables the development of a range of product and process skills, but which may well require staff to carefully induct students into the processes of reflection on learning and peer- and self-assessment processes (Boud 1995; Duch et al., 2001; Stefani, 2004; Tariq et al., 1998).

With regards to enhancing the potential for interdisciplinary/interprofessional programs of study, Lee Shulman (2004) puts forward a proposal for development of "interdisciplinary centres" to overcome faculty intellectual isolation through the creation of new multidisciplinary communities of shared interests and work. Shulman argues that women's studies centres for example, which initially had shaky existences, have often matured into secure interdisciplinary entities such as the Stanford University Institute for Research on Women and Gender.

Interdisciplinary centres, argues Shulman, can provide a home for scholars from a variety of fields who can make possible important new work and the development of new fields of study. This sits well with le Heron's arguments stated above, that interdisciplinarity /transdisciplinarity allows for the combining of intellectual skills to tackle novel problems.

Shulman further suggests that interdisciplinary entities are far more likely to innovate in their teaching and assessment strategies and hints that within individual disciplinary areas curricula are designed according to the individual tastes of faculty members. Moving into interdisciplinary centres allows staff to leave behind certain predispositions (Shulman, 2004). Behind these arguments may lie some indication of the "academic politics" which can provide barriers to realizing the great potential of interdisciplinarity.

Conclusions

It is clear, from an extensive literature survey and discussions with colleagues across a range of disciplines, that there are not many well-developed interdisciplinary/interprofessional programs of study which have been deliberately and coherently developed. Many of the interdisciplinary options available to students are in essence courses which are additive, in that they contain elements of different disciplines. Inevitably, the assessment strategy is unidisciplinary in this context. In other words all of the disciplines represented in the interdisciplinary course will examine or assess learning within the context of their own terrain.

If interdisciplinary programs of study are to be developed in a coherent manner, staff may well have to review their overall concept of assessment of student learning.

It may well be the case that as in the Shapiro (2003) scenario described above, multidisciplinary staff groupings should work in partnership with a facilitator from their educational development unit whose special skill lies in curriculum design and development for program delivery. Frameworks for curriculum design, such as that presented by Cowan and Harding in their 1986 publication "A logical model of curriculum development" or the Biggs model for constructive alignment of teaching, learning, and assessment, are an excellent starting point for encouraging staff to (re)conceptualize what is meant by "the curriculum" as relating to course or program design, development, and delivery (Biggs, 2003).

Staff need to develop a sense of ownership over the curriculum, thus it must be stressed that the models mentioned above are just that, models to be contextualized to the interdisciplinary/interprofessional environment. There may be a need for some serious discussion around learning outcomes or intended learning outcomes. This discussion needs to consider the potential constraints of too much precision around learning outcomes, particularly to move staff away from the notion of content and towards the concept of knowledge, skills, and understanding. Cowan and Harding's model (1986) is particularly helpful in this respect because it persuades staff to consider the "how" and the "what" of assessment (and the author would argue, we need to promote reflection by asking the question "why?" once we consider the "how" and the "what"). How will we assess for the intended learning outcomes? and what will we assess? are questions which allow for an expansion beyond "course content." The questions allow us to ask ourselves what we are really assessing. If, as many educationalists are now advocating, we are ready to make the paradigm shift from assessing knowledge to assessing learning (Broadfoot, 1993) we need to move beyond our comfort zone of seeking "reliability." The "reliability" factor in essence constrains us into comparing students' level of knowledge, which in turn pushes us into norm-referenced assessment. Once we make the bold move of "assessing learning" we need to be much clearer and much more explicit about the criteria against which we are judging students' performance. The criterion-referenced model of assessment actually allows us the freedom to enter into the realms of authentic assessment.

However, authentic assessment will only be appropriate if we are prepared to review the "how" and the "what" of student learning as a next stage in our journey towards interdisciplinary assessment. Will students learn by means of attending lectures, by working in groups to solve "real life" problems, by working as individuals, finding, evaluating, analysing resources, and transforming knowledge? In trying to develop effective assessment strategies, we don't have any choice but to reflect on and review student learning in our courses and programs. This in turn, as Cowan and Harding's model again persuades us, pushes us into reflecting on "how" or "what" we teach, or in current terms, as we consider a further paradigm shift in higher education from a teacher-centered to a learner-centered ethos, the question becomes, how do we facilitate student learning, what resources might we offer? While it is not unproblematic to persuade staff to "buy in" to these paradigm shifts, it is quite unrealistic, given the continually shifting concept of higher education, to continue to try to make "old" practices, suited to a golden age of elitist higher education, fit with the issues presented by mass higher education and the need for greater levels of transformation of knowledge to solve increasingly complex world problems. When we are bold enough to truly embrace the paradigm shifts at departmental and at individual level, our chances of developing and promoting truly interdisciplinary programs of study with appropriate, valid, and authentic assessment strategies will undoubtedly increase dramatically.

References

Ainley, P. (1994). *Degrees of difference: Higher education in the 90's.* London: Lawrence & Wishart.

Becher, T. (1989). *Academic tribes and territories: Intellectual enquiry and the cultures of discipline.* Buckingham: SRHE/Open University Press.

Becher, T., and Trow, P. R. (2001). *Academic tribes and territories* (2nd ed.). Buckingham: SRHE/Open University Press.

Biggs, J. (2003). *Teaching for quality learning at university* (2nd ed.). Buckingham: SRHE/Open University Press.

Boud, D. (1995). *Enhancing learning through self-assessment.* London: Kogan Page.

Boys, C., Brennan, J., Henkel, M., Kirkland, J., Kogan, M., and Youll, P. (1988). *Higher education and preparation for work.* London: JKP.

Breivik, P. A. (1998). *Student learning in the information age.* American Council on Education, Oryx Press.

Broadfoot, P. (1993). Exploring the Forgotten Continent: A traveller's tale, Keynote Lecture, Scottish Educational Research Conference, University of St Andrews, Fife. Published (1994). in *Scottish Educational Review, 26* (2), 88–96.

Cowan, J., and Harding, A. (1986). A logical model of curriculum development. *British Journal of Education Technology, 2*(17), 103–109.

Duch, B. J., Groh, S. E., and Allen, D. E. (Eds.) (2001). *The power of problem-based learning.* Sterling, VA: Stylus.

Elton, L. (2003). *Principles for a fair and honest approach to assessing and representing student's learning and achievement.* Retrieved August 16, 2006, from http://www.ltsn.ac.uk/generi centre/inden.asp?docid=17219.

Everingham, F. (2001). *Undergraduate curricula for professional entry of health science professionals.* Retrieved August 16, 2006 from http://www2.fhs.usyd.edu.au/ugcr/ways_4.htm.

Godfrey, E. (2003). The culture of engineering education and its intersection with gender: A case study of a New Zealand Institution. Ph.D. thesis, Curtin University of Technology.

Hammond, J., and Stefani, L. A. J. (2001). Moving towards an inclusive curriculum at the Glasgow School of Art. *The Skill Journal, 71,* 3–9.

Harris, L. M., and Viney, R. C. (2003). Health science curriculum reform: A framework for evaluation. *Assessment and Evaluation in Higher Education, 28*(4), 411–422.

Henkel, M. (2000). *Academic identities and policy change in higher education.* Higher Education Policy Series No. 45. London: JKP.

Heylings, D. J., and Stefani, L. A. J. (1997). Peer assessment feedback in a large medical anatomy class. *Medical Education, 31,* 281–286.

Higher Education Academy (2006). Retrieved May 16, 2006, from www.heacademy.ac.uk.

Kember, D. (1997). A reconceptualisation of the research into university academics conceptions of teaching. *Learning and Instruction, 7*(3), 255–275.

Knight, P. T., and Yorke, M. (2003). *Assessment, learning and employability.* Buckingham: SRHE/Open University Press.

Lave, J., and Wenger, E. (1991). *Situated learning in legitimate peripheral participation.* Cambridge: Cambridge University Press.

Longworth, N. (1999). *Making lifelong learning work: Learning cities for a learning century.* London: Kogan Page.

Miller, A. H., Imrie, B. W., and Cox, K. (1998). *Student assessment in higher education: A handbook for assessing performance.* London: Kogan Page.

NCIHE (National Committee of Inquiry into Higher Education) (1997). *Higher Education in the Learning Society: Report of the National Committee of Inquiry into Higher Education* (The Dearing Report). London: HMSO.

Prosser, M., and Trigwell, K. (1999). *Understanding learning and teaching: The experience in higher education.* Buckingham: SRHE/Open University Press.

Ramsden, P. (1992, 2003). *Learning to teach in higher education* (1st and 2nd eds). London: Routledge.

Shapiro, D. F. (2002). Improving teaching and learning through outcomes-based capstone experiences. In A. Doherty, T. Riordin, and J. Roth (Eds.), *Student learning: A central focus for institutions of higher education.* A report and collection of institutional practices of the Student Learning Initiative. Milwaukee, WI: Alverno College Institute.

Shapiro, D. F. (2003). Facilitating holistic curriculum development. *Assessment and Evaluation in Higher Education, 28*(4), 423–434.

Shulman, L. (2004). Visions of the possible: Models for campus support of the scholarship of teaching and learning. In W. E. Becker and M. L. Andrews (Eds.), *The Scholarship of Teaching and Learning in Higher Education* (pp. 9–24). Bloomington: Indiana University Press.

Silverman, R., and Welty, W. M. (1996). *An introduction to cases: Center for Case Studies in Education* (Workshop documentation).

Stefani, L. A. J. (2004). Assessment of student learning: Promoting a scholarly approach. *Journal of Learning and Teaching in Higher Education, 1*(1), 51–66.

Tariq, V. N. (2002). A decline in numeracy skills among bioscience graduates. *Journal of Biological Education, 36*(2), 76–83.

Tariq, V. N., Stefani, L. A. J., Butcher, A. C., and Heylings, D. J. A. (1998). Developing a new approach to the assessment of project work. *Assessment and Evaluation in Higher Education, 23*(3), 221–240.

TEDI (2001). *Teaching and Educational Development Institute.* Retrieved July 24, 2006, from http://www.tedi.uq.edu.au.

Wiggins, G. P. (1993). *Assessing student performance.* San Francisco: Jossey-Bass.

5

Understanding "How Students Learn, Both Generally and in the Subject"

SHÂN WAREING

University of the Arts, London

Do students learn differently, depending on the subject discipline they study? Many aspects of the infrastructure of U.K. universities vary according to the answer to this question. For example, do joint honours students have to adopt different ways of learning in their different disciplines? Do some suffer by not adapting sufficiently? Whether students do learn differently in different disciplines is highly relevant to the preparation of university lecturers and their continuing professional development, as if it is the case that there are discipline-based differences in learning it would be important to prepare university lectures for teaching in their specific discipline. If such differences do not exist, then it would be possible to provide effective professional development which dealt with generic principles, theories, and practices of learning.

A debate around the appropriateness of generic preparation for teaching in higher education has been in progress for some time; however, logistical difficulties of providing discipline-based preparation for teaching have meant that few practical experiments have been conducted. The University of Warwick provides a version of its Postgraduate Certificate in Academic and Professional Practice specifically for its mathematicians (Warwick, 2007), and the University of the Arts London (UAL) where this author works provides a Postgraduate Certificate in Learning and Teaching for Art and Design. However, illustrating the kind of logistical difficulties even in an apparently single-discipline higher education institution like UAL, the title was recently changed to "Postgraduate Certificate in Learning and Teaching", due in part to the cosmetic scientists and dancers feeling that the previous title did not adequately encompass their disciplines.

Some readers may be surprised that I raise the question at all of whether students learn differently in different disciplines, because there is high-profile codified evidence of a belief that this is the case. Requirements for national accreditation as a teacher in higher education were first published in the U.K. in 1999 by the Institute for Learning and Teaching in Higher Education and reformulated in 2006 by its successor organization, the Higher Education

Academy (HEA, 2006a). These state that as a requirement of accreditation, staff who teach and support student learning in higher education must demonstrate knowledge and understanding of "how students learn, both generally and in the subject".

Given the accompanying stipulation that teaching practice should be underpinned by scholarship, there is an implication that lecturers will be able to locate a literature to inform their understanding of how students learn in particular subjects. The large number of accredited programs in the U.K. (179 are listed on the Higher Education Academy's website) suggests that accreditors find this requirement to be met. However, it is not readily clear what literature is being referred to, and it is this matter which this chapter attempts to address.

There is a very substantial literature which engages with models of how students learn generically (for example, many accredited courses expect participants to analyze and apply the models of Vygotsky, Piaget, and others).

The recognition of belief in disciplinary difference as a highly significant factor in staff and student motivation is increasingly recognized in the sector, which does see an emerging literature, which considers discipline-specific educational development. The U.K. has established 24 Subject Centres, whose role is in part to interpret generic learning and teaching ideas in the context of the range of disciplines they represent. These have generally been regarded in the sector as successful.

The Subject Centres and resources such as the Supporting New Academic Staff (SNAS) Project, an online database of pedagogic scholarship grouped by subjects, exist partly on the assumption that there are discipline-specific pedagogies which they disseminate. The evidence of this might be expected to be demonstrated through scholarly resources. It is certainly true that there is an increasing body of scholarly work devoted to discipline-based pedagogies. However, it is also the case that generic literature is often cited as part of apparently subject-specific resources. For example, within the SNAS resource (HEA, 2006b), under the subject heading Art, Design, Media and Communication, 33 resources are listed under eight subheadings. Of these, 19 are specific to art, design, media and communication, 13 are generic, and one is partially subject-specific, relating to the broader grouping of humanities.

Not everyone in higher education agrees on the clarity of discipline distinctions though, nor on the usefulness of using disciplines as an organizing principle. The notion of distinct "tribes" and "territories" (Becher) is not accepted universally. There are scholars who critique the assumption that disciplinary boundaries are in any way definable or tangible. Angela Brew has suggested that disciplines are no longer adequate categories for understanding academic practices and subjects. Stephen Rowland has drawn attention to the divisions within disciplines which lead to increasing fragmentation within a subject area. Paul Trowler, co-author of the second edition of *Academic Tribes and Territories*, questions the clarity of discipline distinctions on the basis of, first, differences in apparently identical disciplines between institutions, and second, divisions between disciplines within a single institution.

While the idea of disciplinary difference within higher education has enormous power, there is little tangible evidence for pedagogical differences between disciplines which allow one discipline to be defined pedagogically (rather than by subject material) through contrast with another, or of homogeneity of pedagogy within a discipline which would allow any discipline to define itself in contrast to the external disciplinary environment.

The question of whether there are subject-specific models of student learning in use, with or without a scholarly underpinning, is one which opens up the way the sector understands disciplinary differences in learning and teaching.

Research Methodology

A case study was undertaken with the help of academic staff at a research-led pre-1992 university with approximately 8,000 students. Staff who were undertaking the Postgraduate Certificate in Teaching and Learning or who had recently successfully completed it were asked to provide written answers to four questions:

1. What evidence is there that students in your discipline (or in specific specialist areas within your discipline) learn in a way which is discipline-specific?
2. Regardless of whether you were able to find references to published work or not, do you believe there are differences, and if so, could you indicate what these are?
3. Are there models or theories about student learning which seem particularly suitable to your discipline?
4. Have you any ideas about what a theory or model of student learning should look like or be based on, in order to be useful to academics in your discipline?

There were several purposes in asking academic staff from different departments to participate. It was a means to enlist a number of "research assistants" to improve the extent and depth of the scholarly investigation. In a research-led institution, I relied on academic colleagues having well-developed skills of scholarship which might lead to their discovering resources I might have missed. I also anticipated that they might be familiar with subject-specific resources of which I was unaware. I was curious to see whether staff believed that there were models which were particularly suited to explaining student learning in their disciplines, regardless of whether there was supporting scholarly evidence, and also whether there was something about generic models of student learning which rendered them appropriate or inappropriate in disciplines, which the fourth question was intended to explore.

It was also probable that there would be educational development benefits from conducting the literature searches and reflecting on the responses to the questions, and this was something which could be shared within the institution.

Staff were invited to participate in the study on the basis of having a known interest in pedagogy. I invited 22 members of staff to participate, one from each department. Six written responses were received, from staff in the Departments of Classics, Drama and Theatre Studies, Economics, French, Linguistics, and Physics. It was not intended that the respondents represented the full range of disciplines, nor that they were representative of views within their disciplines.

Results

There was no evidence in the answers of the six respondents of subject-specific models of student learning comparable to the number of generic models of learning in common currency (e.g. Kolb's Learning Cycle; Bloom's Taxonomy; deep and surface approaches to learning, as described by the phenomenographers). Many of the answers focussed on perceived differences in how the subject is taught, rather than about how students of the subject learn. That is, it was assumed that there were differences in how students learnt but these were perceived to occur as a consequence of differences between subjects and subject-teaching practices.

Six propositions came to light which might fit with the Higher Education Academy's requirement to have knowledge and understanding of "how students learn, both generally and in the subject". None of these propositions was as straightforward as the simple statement: "students learn differently in different disciplines", but they were all recognizable, I believe, as givens which are worthy of being integrated into the formal preparation for teaching.

The respondents suggested that:

1. There are differences in the student populations that select to study specific subjects which may lead to different behaviour, different support needs, and consequently differences in learning and teaching practices. For example, if student cohorts studying economics and fine art were compared, respondents expected to find differences in students' motivations in undertaking higher education, in their beliefs about the purpose and process of studying, in aspects of their study preferences, and in the likelihood of their having a specific learning difficulty such as dyslexia.

2. Certain patterns in the prior educational experiences of students entering specific disciplines need to be taken into account in order to design curricula and student support structures which will enable students to learn more effectively. For example, the changing levels of language-learning achieved in schools by students entering modern languages and classics has resulted in changes to the curricula in both

fields, including more extensive *ab initio* language teaching and indeed abolishing the requirement to pass courses in Latin and Greek translation in classics. Teachers of maths, and courses that rely on a maths background such as physics, psychology and, recognise the need to teach maths at an earlier level than previously and take into account students' anxiety around maths.

3. There are specific identifiable concepts ("threshold concepts") and skills within disciplines that students almost always take longer to learn, and these differ between disciplines, but can result in specific emphases or processes being included in the curriculum.

4. Students have expectations of learning and teaching practices when they enrol on a program of study: "Many applied linguistics students are foreign language teachers, and many (especially from the ESL/ESOL profession) practise a 'task-based learning' pedagogy in their role as teachers. I have found that this often creates an expectation of student-centred, multi-sensory pedagogy when they return to the learning environment as students themselves ... Others rapidly become amendable to a 'hands-on' approach, especially where a learning outcome is underpinned by a (difficult) theoretical concept and its relevance to application may be lost in a more traditional lecture-type session" (Applied linguistics respondent). Students are reported to enter higher education expecting to talk more to one another in some disciplines than others.

5. Epistemological differences exist between disciplines, although some of these arguably relate more to the sociological construction of the discipline than its underpinning knowledge structure. However there are clear and immediate differences in expectations of subjectivity and objectivity, between say, fine art, English, economics and physics. Some subjects are taught with an emphasis on kinaesthetics, such as performing arts and, arguably, subjects like geology which have strongly tactile aspects, in comparison with economics for example, where I have observed very little kinaesthetic activity in teaching and learning. The extent to which the subject at undergraduate level emphasizes creativity also varies, although this certainly depends on the definitions of creativity with which one operates. The creative arts tend to foreground creativity (for instance, the University of the Arts has a Centre for Excellence in Teaching and Learning with the title "Creative Learning in Practice"), whereas history, maths, economics tend not to foreground creativity in undergraduate studies to any significant degree (although there are surprises: an MA in Applied Linguistics has "a responsibility to foster creativity in its graduates: to turn them from consumers to producers of linguistically-informed ideas" (Hawkins, 2005). The extent to which the subject focuses on

social learning and group endeavour vs. a set body of knowledge and individual endeavour (drama vs. maths) varies enormously. Some disciplines see learning as primarily cognitive (history, economics) while for others it also includes significant emotional and physical dimensions (drama). There are, similarly, differing views on the extent to which personal experience is perceived to affect learning (this is more emphasized in applied linguistics and drama).

6. The final point is an obvious one: disciplines have different learning and teaching and assessment practices, into which students need to be acculturated (such as labs, practicals, crits., workshops, lectures, problem groups, projects, fieldwork and group presentations).

Discussion and Conclusions

Identity and belonging are powerful underpinning phenomena which influence perception. Linda Drew's work on conceptions of teaching related the most profound "deep" approaches to teaching to a wish on the part of higher education teachers to enable their students to "become a [designer/photographer/other . . .]", or to "become . . . whatever the student wished to become" "Becoming a . . ." (the phrase used on the SNAS website) is shorthand for an underlying philosophy that is increasingly functioning as a powerful model of curriculum intentions and of student learning.

Where academics aspire to "become a . . ." (geographer/historian/mathematician/engineer/biologist . . .), they may perceive this identity to be in contrast with "becoming a teacher". This may result in a difficulty in perceiving the relevance or applicability of generic models of learning, and a receptiveness to models which are perceived to be discipline-based. It has been argued that the identity conflict between being an academic within one's discipline and being a teacher is an unintended but direct result of schemes that reward research excellence in the discipline/subject, such as the Research Assessment Exercise in the U.K., which began to influence institutional behaviour.

The model of disciplinary relationships apparently underpinning my informants' views of teaching is shown in Figure 5.1.

There is a perhaps entirely predictable tendency to attribute all positive characteristics to one's own discipline and all negative attributes to other disciplines (to borrow a term from Said's theory of Orientalism). A model which perhaps more productively explains the pedagogical relationships of the disciplines is Figure 5.2, which shows areas of overlap and difference against a cluster of attributes.

I do not intend to imply that Figure 5.2 adequately indicates all the most significant pedagogic attributes of disciplines, but many of those identified do substantially influence the teaching and learning methods adopted within discipline areas. Plotting one's own discipline against a range of attributes defined by an individual or a team might lead departments within higher

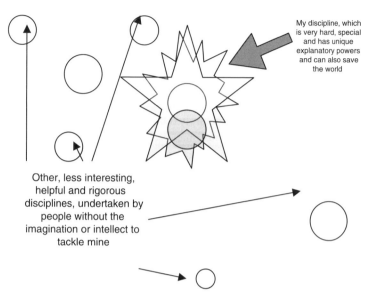

Other, less interesting, helpful and rigorous disciplines, undertaken by people without the imagination or intellect to tackle mine

My discipline, which is very hard, special and has unique explanatory powers and can also save the world

Figure 5.1 Conception of disciplinary relationships—version 1.

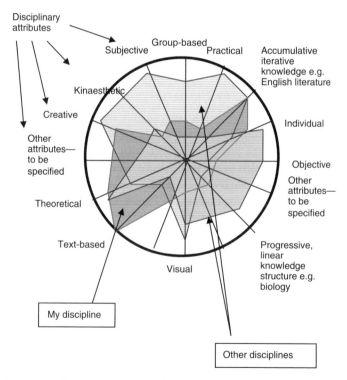

Disciplinary attributes

Subjective

Group-based

Practical

Accumulative iterative knowledge e.g. English literature

Kinaesthetic

Creative

Individual

Other attributes— to be specified

Objective

Other attributes— to be specified

Theoretical

Text-based

Visual

Progressive, linear knowledge structure e.g. biology

My discipline

Other disciplines

Figure 5.2 Conception of disciplinary relationships—version 2.

education institutions to find areas for collaboration and sharing practice which were previously unexplored. Making these aspects of disciplines explicit may help students who move between disciplines and new staff members being inducted into a new department.

The conclusion of this study was that models of learning have a cross-disciplinary applicability despite a tendency to question and criticize generic models of student learning from the perspective of being inapplicable to a particular discipline.

References

Becher, T., and Trowler, P. (2001). *Academic tribes and territories: Intellectual enquiry and the cultures of disciplines* (2nd ed.). Buckingham: Open University Press/SRHE.

Bloom, B. (ed.) (1956). *Taxonomy of educational objectives, the classification of eductional goals – Handbook I: Cognitive domain.* New York: McKay.

Brew, A. (2003). Teaching and research: New relationships and their implications for inquiry-based teaching and learning in higher education. *Higher Education Research and Development 22*(1), 3–18.

Drew, L. (2004). The experience of teaching creative practices: Conceptions and approaches to teaching in the community of practice dimensions in A. Davies (Ed), *Enhancing curricula: Towards the scholarship of teaching in art, design and communication in higher education.* London: Centre for Learning and Teaching (CLTAD), 106–123.

Hawkins, R. (2005). The role of linguistics in the Applied Linguistics MA. Retrieved August 2005, from the Languages and Linguistics Subject Centre website www.llas.ac.uk.

HEA (2006a). Retrieved February 15, 2007, from http://www.heacademy.ac.uk/regandaccr/StandardsFramework(1).pdf.

HEA (2006b). Retrieved February 14, 2007, from http://www.heacademy.ac.uk/SNAS.htm.

Kolb, D. (1984). *Experiential learning: Experience as the source of learning and development.* New Jersey: Prentice-Hall.

Meyer, J. and Land, R. (2005). Threshold concepts and troublesome knowledge (2): Epistemological considerations and a conceptual framework for teaching and learning. *Higher Education 49*(3), 373–388.

Rowland, S. (2002) Overcocming fragmentation in professional life: The challenge for academic development. *Higher Education Quarterly 56*(1), 52–64.

Said, E. (2003). *Orientalism: Western Conceptions of the Orient* (2nd ed.). Penguin: London.

Trowler, P. (forthcoming). *Cultures and change in higher education.* Basingstoke: PalgraveMacmillan.

Warwick (2007). Retrieved February 15, 2007, from http://www2.warwick.ac.uk/fac/sci/maths/pcapp/.

Wenger, E. (1998). *Communities of practice: Learning, meaning and identity.* Cambridge: Cambridge University Press.

6
Cross-Faculty Interdisciplinary Work
How to Work with the "Others"

SUSANA LORENZO-ZAMORANO

University of Manchester

Introduction

Although there is now a history of co-operation among academic staff working on disciplines that somehow complement each other, area studies has not really succeeded in developing all the potentials that interdisciplinarity may have (Klein, 1990, p. 25, quoted in Ellis, 2003, p. 4). As Ellis has noted, this is partly the result "of the limited amount of dialogue between the different Area Studies communities, particularly between those located in Modern European Language Departments and those Area Studies communities centering their work upon other areas of the world" (2003, p. 4). Needless to say, institutional support, time constraints and logistical requirements play an important role in this unequal marriage.

From a modern foreign languages degree point of view, the situation is even less hopeful if we consider the inferior status that language teaching has in many universities in comparison to the other subjects of the same degree (Quist, 2000, p. 124).[1] This is why I claim that languages are therefore put at an initial and clear disadvantage in the so-called interdisciplinary game. Ironically, this handicap is reinforced by the multidisciplinary nature of the traditional approach to language programs curricula development, as it is clear that multidisciplinary working does not guarantee integration and "conjunctive interaction" (Cluck, 1980, p. 68; Klein, 2000, p. 56, quoted in Ellis, 2003) in the way interdisciplinary work theoretically does. Accordingly, in many language departments across the higher education (HE) sector there is still an apparent and illogical divorce between languages and the rest of the subjects and, as a consequence, students seem to have considerable difficulties in relating their "language world" to the other areas in the curriculum. The fact that a substantial number of courses are taught and assessed in English helps little to achieve a more integrated and coherent curriculum. Funnily enough, the most convincing argument put forward for the delivery of content modules in English is precisely that it reaches out to a wider community of students (student recruitment), thus fostering cross-sector activities at the same time as marginalizing once more language teaching and learning.

Whatever the case, it is evident that there is still a lot to do in order to achieve a sound integration of knowledge. This is so much so that the 2003–2004 area studies project[2] identified interdisciplinarity as a key issue (Canning, 2005a, p. 3). The purpose of this chapter is to provide an outline of an experimental interdisciplinary and intercultural course unit at undergraduate level run in 2004–2006 at the University of Manchester involving a degree of interdisciplinarity known as *composite* (Heckhousen, 1972), which denotes the application of multiple disciplines in order to solve societal problems.[3] This credit-rated course unit, incorporating Spanish together with medicine, education, geography and biological sciences, and therefore three faculties (within the institutional structure of the University of Manchester), is based on a successful funded pilot project initially run in 2003.[4] My focus will be to assess the findings of this project in relation to language learning and teaching, and to suggest some implications for the elements of language education itself. My evaluation will be done on the basis of my own qualitative data derived from virtual discussion board threads, the reflective writing in student diaries, the group interviews led by the educational researcher in the staff team, and the actual outcome of student team projects.

I claim that the type of interdisciplinarity in place through our project and our own modus operandi is highly integrative, innovative, and unique to language students, as it not only offers them a *direct* and *meaningful linkage* to today's society—an element somewhat missing in many language programs— but also provides them with maximum exposure to specialized language and involves a real transgression of disciplinary boundaries.

General Description of the Module

The unit, supported by a virtual learning environment (VLE), is modeled on a collaborative enquiry-based learning (EBL) approach in which students work in teams to undertake research on a topic of their own choice leading to a *poster* symposium, which takes place after six weeks. Sample documents together with a framework for action are supplied, the driving force being the selection, by the students, of a starter article that must be both interdisciplinary and focused on a societal or environmental issue, therefore including education for sustainable development as an essential element. The projects involving the Hispanic world so far undertaken include the following subject areas:

- An examination and comparison of waste management in the U.K. and Spain;
- Effects of political violence in Peru, especially in rural communities;
- Road safety in developing countries (Mexico);
- Risks faced by street children in Brazil, especially HIV;

- Legal and socio-political situation of women in Argentina in relation to abortion;
- Effects of TB on the immigrant population in Spain;
- Air pollution in Santiago de Chile.

When presenting their poster students are required to respond to some questions previously posted on the VLE by both the staff and the rest of the teams. The key interdisciplinary element of the course comes in at this stage as every student is to respond to questions from another discipline different from their own. To do this, team mates have to brief each other beforehand. The high level of challenge that this process involves has been acknowledged by the students:

> It has been a hard question to prepare as I have not studied biology since I was 14. . . . But it was challenging to prepare something in which I was not an expert. . . . it was Ana's turn to deal with my lack of knowledge. With lots of patience, she has tried to explain to me step by step the process of landfills and plants, and after an hour of hard work I understood it. It was like a miracle!

After the poster presentation and during the rest of the semester students of Spanish, education and medicine continue working separately for another five extra credits. In the case of Spanish, students are expected to submit three reflective journal entries made while Part 1 was in progress, and further develop a specific research area, including the experience of learning in an interdisciplinary environment itself, on which they make an oral presentation during the last session of the semester.

My specific role in the project has been to develop its virtual component. WebCT was used, as the university's main VLE platform, to ease timetable problems, deliver all the course documents, and as a fundamental support for face-to-face sessions. In this sense it is important to note that some of the tasks are to be submitted as postings to the WebCT discussion board and that both the responses from peers and the feedback from facilitators are done through this virtual environment. WebCT is also used as a pedagogic research tool. For example, the 2005–2006 data on its use prove that the most visited section in our site has been the one containing the sample documents, i.e. the AIDS poster abstract and the poster guidelines.

Role of language students in the project: main challenges and insights. Our language students were expected to bring their own cultural background to bear by relating it to real-life problems and issues. One of my major personal interests in this project was to see to what degree it contributed to the improvement of my students' communicative competence, especially with regard to its linguistic and intercultural component.

Although during the first year we implemented the project, funding and organizational issues prevented an early promotion of the project among the students, I managed to recruit three Spanish Erasmus undergraduates whose degree at their home university basically includes English language and a combination of literature, history and, more broadly, cultural studies dealing with the Anglophone world.[5] In order to better appreciate the benefits of this project, it is important to note that at the end of their degree these students will have normally achieved a deep knowledge of English grammar that does not correspond to their level of fluency in the spoken language.

The two parts of the project work slightly differently depending on the target culture and language of the students recruited. During Part I Erasmus students' exposure to their target language, i.e. English, is both complete and highly complex as it is not simply a different language they are trying to understand and communicate with, but it is also the "language" or jargon of the other disciplines. In other words, all of a sudden this group of students is expected to use Language for Specific Purposes (LSP) or specialized language from different disciplines, something most of them have not done before, at least to this degree.

Consequently, a great part of the reflection that this group of students wrote in their diaries was centered on problems associated with language (losing concentration, correctness, shyness and fear, etc.). Significantly, there was a girl teamed up with two boys, a medic and a geographer, who was particularly concerned about her language performance. She writes:

> I am a bit worried because I feel that the teachers speak a bit fast for me. Although in my home university all my lectures are in English, the lecturers are Spanish or they talk slowly enough so that we all understand easily. However, now my classmates are no more Spanish, neither the teachers, so it seems that I will have to get used to being addressed not as a Spanish studying English but as a "real English student."

> Today has been the first time in my life that I have spoken in English in front of English speakers in a serious context . . . I believe that thinking that my classmates would notice all my mistakes made me feel really nervous and ashamed. The result has been a terrible nonsense speech, which has made me feel really awful.

Likewise, in this first part of the course English native speakers studying Spanish must use their existing knowledge of the target culture and develop their research and analytical skills to a maximum level. More specifically, all our students concur in pointing out how they benefited from acquiring a set of research and study skills they had never used before, i.e. diagrams and concept mapping from geography, and searching journal electronic resources and organizational techniques from medicine.

In contrast with the Spanish native speakers, the demands on our own cohort of students as far as their linguistic skills are concerned are limited to reading and understanding the documentation used for research; this is strongly recommended to be in the target language, although I'm afraid that was not always the case. But even in this part, having to deal with technical language in their own language, English native speakers also find a barrier and end up improving their linguistic competence in their native language.

One of the most striking insights gained in this part of the course is that it proves more difficult for the modern languages student to find a space of their own in the group. This could stem from the fact that some disciplines are considered "weaker" in terms of their applications or practicalities. As one of our students states:

> This kind of idea rises from a very materialistic point of view whereby human beings are only considered physical entities and their spiritual, artistic, intellectual and even psychological aspects are forgotten or answered to with material solutions.

Spanish became peripheral to him only accidentally, when he found that the relationship with Spain of the so-called Spanish flu, referring to the 1918 outbreak, was anecdotal.

In some cases it is the nature of some disciplines that makes them overlap, as one of the student records, referring to geography and Spanish and the topics of demography, immigration, and society. However, in other instances it is the insecurity that the student feels about their own discipline which leaves their castle vulnerable and makes the definition of roles difficult. This problem again supports the idea of the perceived fragmentation within their own degree and finds a correlation with the difficulty that these students experience in the initial ice-breaker activity, which consists of defining their own discipline to the others. "It is hard to explain which is the objective of studying literature and linguistics," one student states.

During the rest of the semester, when our students are to expand upon the experiences and project that they have been working on within their inter-disciplinary team, the means of communication is Spanish. This naturally demands more of an effort on the part of the English native speakers, who are now expected to use their target language as a means of communication and thus contribute to expanding the project using the same varieties of specialized language that the non-native speakers of English use in Part I. Reflection in the target language in the case of the former group of students was not very satis-factory in terms of the use of language and, thus, I have learned that the purely linguistic correctness in the target language needs to be emphasized more as an objective among English students in the second part.

It must be noted that when it comes to learning a language, both the lin-guistic and the socio-cultural competence needed are relatively easy to acquire. However, the fact that only a very small proportion of students succeeds in achieving the intercultural competence[6] after their year abroad says a lot about the complexity of the latter. In this sense, I am glad to say that apart from the linguistic and skill gains so far pointed out, this project has made significant accomplishments in helping our students to become more intercultural, to be more sensitive to differences, and this had an impact on their negotiation skills. Thus, one of the most highly rated aspects of the course both in the evaluation form and the students' reflective diaries lay precisely in seeing problems from a different perspective. This is of extreme importance, as intercultural competence is indeed the most challenging aspect of both teaching and learning a foreign language.

However, it is not just a question of language. Any institution that includes internationalization among its goals by default aims at producing cross-culturally competent students or global citizens. Are we really doing this? It is interesting to note the one-way system that is currently in place and that has been highlighted by Deardorff referring to the U.S. institutions of HE, which "rely heavily on numbers to demonstrate success in internationalization" (Deardorff, 2004, p. 14). But having just one unit of measurement is not enough. While we are happy to receive, we are failing to give what we are supposed to in an economically and culturally globalized world. This is why the American Council on Education has advised all those institutions that are serious about their international status to "take a closer look at learning goals, course content, pedagogy, campus life, enrolment pattern, and institutional policies and practices" (Engberg and Green, 2002, quoted in Deardorff, 2004, p. 14). I claim that our project has greatly developed this competence, especially more so in the case of our first cohort of students, who had to deal with both their own discipline-related world or culture and that of the other disciplines together with their identity-related culture and that of the others.[7] The empathy and respect toward different cultures is manifest in the following comment:

> When we started to compare Thailand with Spain I felt that some kind of western pride arose talking about the Thai people, clouded by superstitions and far from our scientific advance. Are we giving birth to a new fundamentalism? Is science the new religion of the West? I felt a bit afraid when I realized that we were regarding science as the unique truth and discarding other beliefs.

But in order to become intercultural speakers, students are to move beyond that initial empathy stage, "decentre" from their own culture (Byram et al., online, 7) and develop a capability to navigate different ways of thinking and discourses. Through mediation and negotiation skills students are ideally meant to construct a "third space" (Bhabha, 1992, p. 58) between identities and cultures. This process of relativization of one's own values, beliefs and behaviors (Byram et al., online, 7) was evidenced, for example, when one of our students, defending abortion in the context of Argentina, had a different perspective on it after she was briefed by the medic on the details of the process. Not that she changed her mind as a consequence, but she succeeded in acquiring a more integrative perspective that incorporated all the different angles and was very capable of acting as a mediator. In her journal she reflected on the sensitivity of an issue that for some people is narrowly linked to religion (and it just happened that the medic was a Muslim). She also remarked on how the medic, who believed there was a precise and exact answer to everything, realized the benefit of incorporating different perspectives.

Additionally, as Canning points out, "intercultural competence is not only concerned with the engagement across geographical space, but it can also be a bridge to translate the disciplinary gap between the humanities and the sciences" (2005b, p. 15). Canning emphasizes the need to find a type of language that is more accessible in order to incorporate education for sustainable development into disciplines that are not necessarily sciences. This accommodation of different languages is thus a characteristic of interdisciplinarity (Heintz and Origgi, 2006) as well as a means to develop intercultural competence. The following are some students' comments that prove the development of their interculturality:

> It's going to help me if I qualify to be a doctor talking to everyday public who are not aware of the medical jargon so you've got to talk in everyday words to explain to them.

> If you're talking to someone from a non-specialist background you've got to be as simple as possible for them to understand what you're trying to communicate and I think that's a big lesson I've learned.

So do the atoms always connect into compounds? Of course not! The "other" was still the "other" for some students at the end of the project in spite of their valuable gains in other areas. After some evaluative research mainly based on both the group interviews and the reflective diaries, our conclusions on the performance of individual students and their teams consider the following key factors:

- The nature of the module depending on the discipline, which greatly affects the degree of motivation: students of medicine do it on a compulsory basis;
- Students' personality, which determines the team roles and dynamics;
- The degree of self-confidence that each of them possessed in their own discipline;
- Stereotypes about the other disciplines such as the one illustrated by this comment from a geographer: "I was really impressed with the languages people. They don't just study the language and we don't just study maps."

Thus stereotypes may act as important unseen interferences and affect the team dynamics a great deal, impeding communication and putting at risk everything else. In fact, this project has given us a greater insight into the role of stereotypes in the teaching and learning process. As a result, our recommendation for a generic unit would include more time at the very early stages dedicated to identifying stereotypes and other manifestations of discrimination and prejudice, and calling into question preconceptions about the other disciplines. This would contribute to fostering intercultural competence to a greater degree.

Conclusion

The results of being part of this project are paramount in the sense that, with relation to language teaching and learning, they have meant:

- New perspectives to language learning (perspectives not just limited to literature, history or, more broadly, cultural studies, but incorporating more disparate disciplines such as medicine and biological sciences);
- Implementation of a new type of communicative methodology in the teaching of foreign languages that manages to achieve a reasonable balance of language, culture, and, what is most important, interculturality;
- Considerable improvement of our students' communicative competence at various levels including the acquisition and development of intercultural skills;
- Acquisition and enhancement of various hands-on skills including collaborative, communicative, analytical, critical, and creative ones;
- A strengthening of the existing Study Abroad program and departmental curriculum.

For reasons to do with institutional constraints, I am dubious about the possibility of embedding this modality of teaching and learning on a larger scale unless appropriate support is put in place. On the other hand, I believe that attempts to promote interdisciplinarity depend very much upon how well interrelated the different components of a discipline are. In our particular case, there is still a lot to be done to put languages where they deserve to be and achieve a more integrated curriculum at departmental level before we engage in cross-faculty interdisciplinarity. It is a question of achieving consensus on this first among ourselves before attempting to make new friends.

Language is not only the "primary activity" (Towell, 2005, p. 13) in modern foreign languages departments but I do believe it is key not only to the construction of culture but to the emergence of cultural change, and this role of language tutors as "agents of social change" (Kramsch, 1997, p. 7) is often neglected and even ignored by language tutors themselves. In fact, attempts to devise pedagogical applications of this approach are still scarce. Because of this, and despite the above remarks, I would like to encourage projects like ours for various reasons: it has helped us to deepen our pedagogical understanding to a great extent and therefore has proved invaluable for future program planning. Apart from providing our students with a valuable package of skills, it makes disciplines come together, talk, and be enriched through their dialog. Additionally, it has the potential of being a powerful tool to measure the effectiveness of the internationalization of our institutions. Its interdisciplinary nature is a means for us and our students to become intercultural, have a better understanding of the world, and ideally act accordingly. Therefore, I believe that it is our duty as educators in the context of multicultural societies to promote this kind of initiative, even with all its faults and deficiencies, and to disseminate it and learn from it so that more perfected models may appear. In other words, the crossing of the artificial borders between disciplines should be encouraged in HE institutions at all costs. Even individually, disciplines should try to engage more with certain environmental and societal topics that fall outside their classical domain. Modern languages are no exception and the Hispanic world is a mine of information in this sense.

Acknowledgments

I would like to thank Julia McMorrow, from the School of Geography, Charlotte Woods, from the School of Education at the University of Manchester, both members of the project team, and Jocelyn Wyburd, from the University of Manchester Language Centre, for their helpful comments on this chapter.

Notes

1. Language is not considered a priority area of research in many institutions either. According to Professor Towell, "our universities may be in danger of becoming the only major businesses which fund little or no research into their primary activity: specialised teaching and learning" (2005, p. 13). Quist also refers to other indicative elements such as staffing levels and terms of employment (2000, p. 125).
2. A partnership between the Centre for Languages, Linguistics and Area Studies (LLAS) and five other Subject Centres funded by the Learning and Teaching Support Network (LTSN). Although the Area Studies Project concluded in 2004, LLAS is now developing the project's outcomes further (Canning, 2005a, p. 5).
3. The project actually started in 2003 and has been running for three years now. I joined in 2004.
4. For two consecutive years (2003–2005) the project was financed by the Teaching and Learning Support Unit Curriculum Innovation Fund, and this year (2005–2006) by the Centre for Excellence in Enquiry-Based Learning (CEEBL).
5. The fact that no English students expressed any interest was perhaps an indicator that our second years, for whom the project was originally destined, could not make sense of what an interdisciplinary module was about. As a consequence, the following year I developed a more detailed module description on the project and, also because of the intercultural element involved in it, I also decided that the best target audience was final year students that had already spent a year abroad.

6. According to the Common European Framework, intercultural skills include: the ability to relate the culture of origin and the foreign culture to each other; the capacity to fulfil the role of intermediary between one's own culture and the foreign culture and to deal effectively with intercultural misunderstanding; and the ability to overcome stereotyped relationships (Council of Europe, 2001, p. 104). For more on this see Byram (2003).
7. The latter would comprise the elements applied by Lázár et al. (2001, pp. 5–6) to language teaching, i.e. civilization, behavior and speech patterns, and text structure and skills.

References

Bhabha, H. K. (1992). Post-colonial authority and post-modern guilt. In L. Grossberg, C. Nelson, and P. Treichler (Eds.), *Cultural Studies* (pp. 56–66). London: Routledge.

Byram, M. (2003). *Intercultural competence.* Strasbourg: Council of Europe.

Byram, M., Gribkova, B., and Starkey, H. (n.d.). Developing the intercultural dimension in language teaching. Retrieved October 28, 2006, from http://lrc.cornell.edu/director/intercultural.pdf.

Canning, J. (2005a). Leading the way in interdisciplinary teaching and learning. Subject Centre for Languages, Linguistics and Area Studies. *LLAS Digest*, pp. 3–5.

Canning, J. (2005b). Education for sustainable development. *LLAS Digest*, 14–15.

Cluck, N. A. (1980). Reflections on the interdisciplinary approach to the humanities. *Liberal Education*, 66(1), 67–77.

Council of Europe (2001). *Common European framework of reference for languages: Learning, teaching, assessment.* Cambridge: Cambridge University Press.

Deardorff, D. K. (2004). Internationalization: In search of intercultural competence. *International Educator*, 13–15.

Ellis, R. J. (2003). Interdisciplinarity. Retrieved August 22, 2005, from http://www.lang.ltsn.ac.uk/resources/goodpractice.aspx?resourceid=1430.

Engberg, D., and Green, M. (2002). *Promising practices: Spotlighting excellence in comprehensive internationalization.* Washington, DC: American Council on Education.

Heckhousen, H. (1972). Discipline and interdisciplinarity. In H. Heckhousen (Ed.), *Interdisciplinarity: Problems of teaching and research in universities* (pp. 83–89). Organization for Economic Co-operation and Development.

Heintz, C., and Origgi, G. (2006). Rethinking interdisciplinarity. Emergent issues. *Interdisciplines.* Retrieved July 7, 2006, from http://www.interdisciplines.org/interdisciplinarity/papers/11.

Klein, J. T. (1990). *Interdisciplinarity: History, theory and practice.* Detroit: Wayne State University Press.

Klein, J. T. (2000). A conceptual vocabulary of interdisciplinary science. In P. Weingart and N. Stehr (Eds.), *Practising interdisciplinarity* (pp. 3–24). Toronto: Toronto University Press.

Kramsch, C. (1997). The cultural component of language teaching. *British Studies Now, 8*, 4–7.

Lázár, I., with Aleksandrowicz-Pedich, L., Kjartansson, R., and Skopinskaja, L. (2001). *Workshop report 2/2001: Incorporating intercultural communicative competence in pre- and in-service language teacher training.* Graz: ECML.

Quist, G. (2000). Language teaching at university: A clash of cultures. *Language and Education, 14*(2), 123–139.

Towell, R. (2005). Pedagogic research and the RAE. *LLAS Digest*, 13–14.

Further Reading

The Interdisciplinary Journal of Problem-Based Learning. Retrieved October 28, 2006, from http://docs.lib.purdue.edu/ijpbl/.

Association for Integrative Studies. Retrieved October 28, 2006, from http://www.units.muohio.edu/aisorg/.

Lee Dubrow, G. (2003). Interdisciplinary approaches to teaching, research, and knowledge: A bibliography (http://www.grad.washington.edu/Acad/interdisc_network/ID_Docs/bibliography_Interdisc.pdf, last accessed on 28/10/06).

7

Staff Development for Interdisciplinary Programs

GWEN VAN DER VELDEN

University of Bath

There are many universities—and especially those established in the 1960s—that consider interdisciplinarity to be an important element of their academic identity. Higher education (HE) stakeholders, such as employers, students, or policy makers, also influence the drive towards interdisciplinarity. Stakeholders from within the HE sector, whether driven by interdisciplinary research interests, by a need for expansion of student numbers, or by a desire to translate the needs of a complex society by a broader offer of curricula, also drive the interdisciplinary agenda forward. Interestingly, since the increased efforts to encourage progression between further and higher education, there has also been pressure from the FE sector to widen not just student access, but also to broaden the curriculum patterns and choices available. For these and a number of other reasons, interdisciplinarity is a principle that is increasingly present in curriculum (or program or course) development. In the process of shaping HE in line with the expectations of all these different stakeholders, staff and educational developers have a role to play.

The Role of the Discipline in Staff Development

In the field of staff and educational development itself, both discipline-specific and cross-disciplinary (generic) approaches are commonly used. Staff and educational developers often view cross-disciplinary engagement as a benefit of their work to those who receive their support. Learning from academic colleagues and students how an educational challenge is dealt with differently, due to different subject characteristics, or due to different problem-solving approaches that subject specialists have, often helps developers understand the core of the problem better, as well as understanding more of the principled ways of thinking within a discipline context. Many academic staff taking part in development projects or cross-disciplinary staff development activities will also register the advantages of learning from practices in other disciplines. Although valuable, cross-disciplinary comparison does not constitute linkage of the disciplines that one would expect when wishing to achieve interdisciplinarity. It is less usual that true interdisciplinary engagement is supported in traditional staff and educational development, than that cross-disciplinary (or "generic") learning is. In the case of interdisciplinary education, specific, customized approaches to teaching and assessment will be even more sought after than generic teaching solutions.

The transfer of processes, procedures, and practices transferred from one discipline to another may be viewed as an instance of cross-disciplinary engagement. However, "interdisciplinarity" in this chapter *only* refers to contexts where the discipline content of one discipline engages with another in new processes or activities.

Whilst on the issue of use of terminology, the term "staff development" in this chapter encompasses both the supported learning of staff responsible for the academic learning of students, and the development of the educational process in which these staff are involved (Kahn and Baume, 2003). It is not used to describe a form of training whereby "the right approach" is signalled, or in which staff are expected to accept assumptions or approaches without discussion. Some staff development may include briefing and raising awareness of (teaching) methods, approaches, or systems, but it will also usually entail in-depth analysis of such approaches and evaluation of their appropriateness for actual use in the academic context of learning (be it discipline-specific or not). It is obvious that staff will benefit from contact with others from a mix of discipline backgrounds, as this will help to stimulate the contrasting, comparison, and discussion of disciplinary practices in learning sessions. Incidentally, when considering staff development to help promote interdisciplinarity and implement it effectively, such development opportunities can just as well be led by program or academic leaders as by professional staff and educational developers.

Staff and Educational Development Areas for Interdisciplinarity

Beyond the development of the actual curriculum for an interdisciplinary program, interdisciplinarity also has educational development impacts in a large number of non-curricular areas. Many of the educational challenges raised below are typically the questions staff and educational developers—if not the academic staff themselves—will raise at some point during the process of offering an interdisciplinary education. They may be addressed in consultations with academic staff at the time of curriculum design, or in staff development workshops, or through other routes. Especially the wider questions of a more philosophical nature are likely to be raised in a teaching training program for new academic staff (Post Graduate Certificate in Higher Education or similar).

Broadly the topics fall into four groups: those affecting teaching and assessment (A), those affecting students (B), those relating to curriculum design (C), and the educational and philosophical consideration of interdisciplinarity (D).

A: Staff Development Regarding the Use of Teaching and Assessment Methods for Interdisciplinary Learning

Where a role-playing or lab-based workshop may be appropriate in one discipline, it can be obviously inappropriate in another. Likewise a traditional unseen exam can be right for one course, but would be an invalid form of assessment in another. Ideally, choices of teaching and assessment methods are chosen on the basis of the learning needs defined in intended learning outcomes and the study methods of the students (Winter, 2004 or Biggs, 2003). It then follows that each course or module that carries its own learning outcomes should be offered and tested using particular teaching and assessment means. This then raises the question whether this should be done with or without considering alignment or coherence of methods across the modules or courses that make up a full curriculum or program.

Indeed, variety of teaching and assessment methods is generally experienced as a positive factor, as long as teaching and assessment methods across the curriculum do not conflict with each other, and no confusion is caused by the different approaches. For those courses or modules that bridge two or more subjects (and are possibly co-taught), it is important that there is a full understanding by staff of the ranges of methods that either subject community uses. A common first step in staff development is therefore raising awareness of how different the study and assessment habits of students within different academic disciplines are, and this may hugely surprise staff. Usually such staff development takes the approach of an exchange or showcase of methods, by using examples from modules or assessments that are in use already.

Following on from this, staff developers will want to help their academic colleagues concentrate particularly on the role of a particular method, and the reasons for selecting that method. It can for instance be worthwhile comparing the use of seemingly the same assessment methods, by comparing the role of such an assessment in the overall expected learning process of students. Examples of such evaluation of methods are: Is this test used as formative or summative assessment? Is the purpose of the timing of these oral presentations to generate feedback and learning, or are they used to inspire students to really engage with the text they present on?

The next area of development is to develop a manner of effectively evaluating choices and making decisions between different educational methods, at the design stage of interdisciplinary learning. Important to note is that as long as students are clear on what is expected of them in a given learning situation, and such expectations are made explicit, there is no proven need to "homogenize" teaching, learning, or assessment methods. A common finding at this stage is the importance of developing teaching or assessment methods that combine the best of both disciplines, or new methods to allow for effective learning, teaching, or assessment across disciplines.

Part and parcel of this stage has to be the design of educational evaluation means, to test and analyze the effectiveness of the chosen methods, after these have been implemented.

Finally, the knowledge gained from the development of interdisciplinary learning can lead to innovation in disciplinary teaching. Is there perhaps value in transferring teaching and assessment methods or organizational approaches specifically designed for interdisciplinary programs to disciplinary learning? Or to put it differently: What can strictly disciplinary teaching staff learn from staff that teach in an interdisciplinary program? At this point, the academic colleague that started out as a "staff learner" can take on the role of staff "developer," and share relevant experiences of how such transfer of methods could be possible.

B: Staff Development in Support of Interdisciplinary Student Learning

If students work within the educational context of two subjects where educational approaches are relatively closely associated (say two subjects within the broad realm of social sciences), it may not be necessary to pay much explicit attention to teaching or assessment methods, because they are reasonably alike. But if students are undertaking modules from say a science subject and a humanities subject, teaching, learning, and assessment methods may be very different indeed. Unless a high level of communality between teaching and assessment methods is established within the design of the interdisciplinary curriculum (and the desirability of this may well be questionable [Knight, 2000], teaching staff will have to become very explicit about their learning and assessment expectations of students, as they cannot assume that students will already be accustomed to what is "normal" learning and study for the subject. Some staff learning may need to take place about how to make study and assessment expectations explicit, although it is more likely that educational development will take the shape of planning coherent and integrated student learning guidance and cross-discipline tutorial support (as well as remedial support) by staff from across the disciplines involved.

In certain programs, the element of interdisciplinarity is so essential to the academic value of the program as a whole that explicit attention needs to be paid to exploring the value of the interdisciplinarity by students. As an example, in multimedia studies, where students combine the subjects of electronics, computing, visual arts, and sometimes psychology, it is crucial for students to understand how parts of each of these subjects together make up their chosen interdisciplinary subject of multimedia studies. For academic staff and staff developers the question then is to design new ways or consider and adjust existing ways of helping students learn about or experience this, which can be complicated if the individual teaching staff themselves have a strong affiliation with only one of the disciplines.

Staff and educational developers—or academic leaders themselves—can support the process by collating examples of good practice available through HE Academy Subject Centres, professional bodies, educational literature, and other means commonly available and used by educational professionals.

As in the case of teaching and assessment methods, the quality of student learning advice, certainly if newly designed, will need to be evaluated. Staff development on appropriate means of evaluation for student support (such as focus groups, questionnaires, or nominal group techniques [see Harvey, 1998 for more methods] may also be needed.

C: Staff Development in Support of Curriculum Design

Whilst taking into account what level of interdisciplinarity is chosen for the curriculum, academic leaders and staff developers have to resolve with the relevant teaching team whether and how staff teaching on interdisciplinary programs are to become aware of the academic content addressed in parts of the course that fall outside their expertise. Academic teams or their leaders may need to define to what level of detail and depth do teaching staff need to be aware of interdisciplinary content themselves, and to what extent do differences in teaching and assessment methods per discipline have an influence on their "need to know." In short: does the learning by teaching staff have to be "as interdisciplinary" as it will be for their students?

These are not easy questions to answer, and are highly dependent on the level of integration that is chosen within the interdisciplinary curriculum.

Roughly, there are three types of interdisciplinary curriculum development that staff developers could consider supporting: The inclusion of study of other than the core subject in a course or program, the design of a curriculum that consists of more than one explicitly defined subject, or the fully integrated degree program.

The most common form, especially in arts, humanities, and social sciences, is the approach to allow or encourage their students to take elective courses or wild card modules from other disciplines. The assumption is that students will benefit from a wider academic knowledge than that which is offered strictly within their own discipline.

The staff developer will need to explore whether the teaching team they work with feels that interdisciplinarity is more appropriate for student learning in the early phases of their learning (say in the first year of their program), or whether students are expected to first develop a firm footing in a single discipline before they can fully appreciate intellectually the value of the different nature of another discipline (i.e., in the final stages of their studies).

This level of interdisciplinarity does not necessarily mean that the interaction between different subjects is encouraged in the design of curricula, assessments, or teaching methods. Especially in modularized and credit-based systems such interaction can be difficult to cater for. This particularly is an area where staff development activities can be used to provide creative approaches to interdisciplinary engagement of learning and teaching methods, or even simply to raise awareness of the issue of the intellectual integration of subjects. Staff and educational developers can take a supportive role in collating an overview of approaches to interdisciplinary teaching, learning, and assessment, using examples from other programs. They can also glean ideas from other universities by using established staff development exchange networks (such as the Staff and Educational Development Association, SEDA) or the experience and knowledge available through the Subject Centres of the HE Academy or professional bodies.

Joint or combined discipline degrees take the cross-disciplinary approach a step nearer to actual interdisciplinarity as it allows students to take two (or more) disciplines in conjunction as part of their overall academic study, whilst allowing the student the choice—up to a point—of which disciplines are combined. It will depend on the design of both parts of the joint program whether any engagement between the different disciplines will take place. Of course, it is expected that the learner will make cross-disciplinary connections, but it is a matter for discussion whether the disciplinary engagement should be promoted in the design of the separate parts of the joint program (beyond the final year project or thesis) or not. That discussion could well be supported by staff development activities at the time of the design of a joint curriculum. Further staff development may be desirable at the point of deciding how learning, teaching, or assessment methods should promote an interdisciplinary approach to mastering more than one subject, and these are described elsewhere in this chapter.

The main question staff developers should ask academic staff developing such joint programs is what they aim to achieve by the combination of two or more disciplines. The initial argument for combining disciplines that can be selected by the student—as opposed to the design of a degree program with disciplines *specified* by academic staff—will have included some discussion of what the aim of the combined program is. By returning to those considerations and aims, it can be established what level of integration between disciplines is desired. Following on from that, further attention can be paid to how to achieve such integration.

Sometimes fully interdisciplinary degree programs are developed which, over time, result in co-disciplinary subjects that become disciplines in themselves. An example from the 1950s and 1960s was computing, now a discipline in itself, but at the time often established out of the combination of electronics and mathematics. Following on from this development, computing discipline combined with cognitive psychology (or parts thereof) leading to the new area of artificial intelligence. In both cases, the initial "merger" between the two disciplines may have started in combined research, but was quickly followed by academic study programs. Since the late nineties similar developments can be observed in the areas of forensic sciences or multimedia studies.

However interesting such developments are to follow (see also Becher, 1994), it is more common for staff developers to be supporting new interdisciplinary programs that are not yet developed within a context of a reasonably established—although new—subject area.

For universities where teaching is explicitly research-led there is an additional set of questions that need to be considered in a staff development context: How are (non-) interdisciplinary research-related learning outcomes addressed in the curriculum? How do students learn research methods that are appropriate for the entirety of the interdisciplinary field they are studying? If there is a final project, especially at masters level, will the research element be taught in a discipline-specific, interdisciplinary way? If so, what exactly constitutes the minimum level of "interdisciplinarity" of a project topic? How are links made to existing research in progress at the university, which may or may not be of an interdisciplinary nature? See also the work of Blackwell and Blackmore (2003) for a further exploration of research-led teaching or Brew (2002) for an exploration of research-led educational development.

D: Topics of a Philosophical Nature

The main educational question to be raised by staff and educational developers is exactly what the value of interdisciplinarity is to the relevant academic community of staff and students. A teaching team may or may not conclude that interdisciplinarity in itself has an educational value which is to be promoted. What this will mean in practice will of course depend on the formal mission of the university, or the choices individual academics responsible for programs wish to make, or indeed, the students who may desire to specialize in a narrow subject field or aim for a wider-ranging approach.

Ultimately, the answering of this question will be the responsibility of the academic community who own the higher education programs they offer, in the context of the university which may or may not have taken an explicit stance on interdisciplinarity. Certainly if the formal university policy has not come forward out of recent internal discussion and consultation, it is worthwhile for staff developers and teaching teams to explore the views of academic staff involved in interdisciplinary programs. It will help find common ground between different stakeholders in interdisciplinary development, and support the development of a—hopefully shared—sense of interdisciplinary direction.

If interdisciplinarity is felt to be of a desirable educational or philosophical value, staff development could help a teaching team establish what their shared view is regarding the level and locus of control over discipline choice. In practice this means that the team explores whether it is felt that students should be given freedom in choosing the different subjects, or whether they should be steered. Taking the latter stance to its fullest extent, a teaching team may take the view that teaching staff should themselves specify subject combinations for students, as at least they may already have engaged with both subjects in substantial detail and can make the best-informed choices about the value and use of discipline combinations.

The much larger and more academically philosophical question that may be appropriate for an HE teacher training program or an HE continuing development program is whether it is desirable that interdisciplinary ventures that greatly benefit from the freedom that comes with a lack of singular subject boundaries can become a new subject in themselves. Or to what extent can interdisciplinary teaching serve as an intermediate stage in the more or less organic development of new subject disciplines? For this type of question, it may be less relevant to discuss interdisciplinarity as an educational issue, as the growth of a new singular subject area can of course also come forward primarily out of interdisciplinary research development. Such a broad question concentrates learners' minds on how academic communities are built, grow, and develop. In some cases it can also help individuals learn about their own positioning towards academic research, development, and education, in terms of taking a specialist approach, a broadening view, or multilateral stance. For those readers able to read Dutch and with an interest in sociology and interdisciplinary development, please refer to Peschar and Wesselingh (1985).

References

Becher, T. (1994). The significance of disciplinary differences. *Studies in Higher Education, 19*(2), 151–161.

Biggs, J. (2003). *Teaching for quality learning at university.* Buckingham: The Society for Research into Higher Education and the Open University Press.

Blackwell, R., and Blackmore, P. (Eds.) (2003). *Towards strategic staff development in higher education.* Buckingham: Society for Research into Higher Education and the Open University Press.

Brew, A. (2002). Towards research-led educational development. *Exchange 3,* 25–26.

Harvey, J. (1998). LTDI evaluation cookbook. *Learning Technology Dissemination Initiative.* Edinburgh: Heriot-Watt University.

Kahn, P. E., and Baume, D. (Eds.) (2003). *A guide to staff and educational development.* London: Kogan Page.

Knight, P. T. (2000). The value of a program-wide approach to assessment. *Assessment and Evaluation in Higher Education, 25*(3), 237–251.

Peschar, J. L., and Wesselingh, A. A. (Eds.) (1985). Onderwijs Sociologie, een inleiding. Groningen: Wolters-Noordhoff.

Winter, R. (2004). Contextualising the patchwork text: Addressing problems of coursework assessment in higher education. In R. Winter, J. Parker, and P. Ovens, The patchwork text: A radical re-assessment of coursework assignments. *Innovations in Education and Teaching International Special Issue, 40*(2), 112–122.

8

Work-Based Learning as Interdisciplinary Study

A Discussion of Pedagogy and Practice

KATE IRVING

University of Chester

To be a successful participant in today's world requires a complex set of personal, intellectual, and practical skills: life is an "interdisciplinary" experience. Rapid advances in society and in the diversity of work roles—paid, voluntary, and domestic—require us all to be able to respond to change and to understand and learn from the ways in which knowledge is constructed in a range of different contexts.

This chapter will explore how a pedagogy for work-based learning can enable students to develop skills to understand and develop their own capability, and to capture the "tacit knowledge" that resides in the complexity of the workplace. Firstly, the notion of "interdisciplinarity" is considered in relation to the context of work-based learning. A review of factors that are leading to the increased significance of work-based learning in higher education is considered in the light of interdisciplinary study and the demands on current and future higher education provision. A particular pedagogic approach to developing students' learning in workplace situations is presented, followed by a discussion of how this can be transferred to other contexts, including interdisciplinary studies in academic settings. It is argued that the specific skills developed through engaging with a developed work-based learning pedagogy enables students to learn more effectively in all situations, whether on programs of study or not, and, more importantly, to sustain the capacity for lifelong learning.

The concept of "interdisciplinary studies" has a variety of interpretations. However, as Shearer (2007) has identified, most definitions in the research literature incorporate the idea of learning both within and across discipline boundaries, and the creation of "new knowledge" as a result, often building on, and gaining strength from, the shared and contrasting epistemologies of the disciplines concerned. When these ideas are considered in relation to learning through work, the range of "subjects" that impact on the workplace define it as a site of interdisciplinary study, for example, in theories of interpersonal communication and personal learning, with their roots in psychology and sociology, and in business and management, founded on economics. Add to this the "core activity" of the workplace, and the breadth of disciplines that are involved becomes even more apparent. Not all participants in the workplace believe, of course, that they "need to know" about the wider issues that impact on their work. However, those who understand how an organization operates and appreciate the external context in which it is situated are more effective as workers and, as a result, have greater potential to progress in their careers. This surely, should also be an aim for those who plan outcomes for graduates of higher education programs.

Work-based learning within university curricula is receiving more attention than ever before in higher education in the U.K. Economic and political demands on the higher education (HE) sector require it to become more responsive to the needs of the wider society that it serves. Widening participation continues to be supported as a means of meeting the increased demand for higher level skills and knowledge in the workplace. As Brennan and Little (2006) have argued, this requires higher education institutions (HEIs) to reconsider the boundaries between higher education and employment, and indeed they observe "that boundaries are becoming blurred between the knowledge acquired within educational settings and knowledge acquired in social contexts" (p. 6). This suggests that the concept of interdisciplinarity not only applies to learning across academic disciplines, but also to learning that links disciplinary study with learning through work, and to the development of pedagogies that facilitate learning in integrated, complex contexts.

The development of particular pedagogies for work-based learning has taken place in a number of U.K. HEIs. For some time, research literature has explored the concepts involved, as in the work of Boud and Solomon (2001). At the University of Chester a period of work placement activity has been an integral part of undergraduate degree programs in the second year of full-time study since the early 1980s. This provision has become a key aspect of the university's undergraduate curriculum, with the work-based learning and its assessment being contained within the framework for academic credit. In parallel with the continual evolution and extension of work-based learning opportunities to other employer-based programs at this HEI, a particular pedagogical approach to the design and assessment of this learning opportunity has developed (Brodie and Irving, 2007). The principles inherent in this pedagogy form the basis for framing both the learning and teaching strategy, and the students' assessment within the work-based learning module. In gaining recognition for both the academic credit for this learning and through the development of the underpinning pedagogy, both student and staff perceptions are enabled to move from the concept of this experience as a "work placement" to that of it being a valuable opportunity for higher-level learning, with links to both the development of "employability skills" and for the development of skills for final year undergraduate study, particularly in relation to the skills of critical analysis. As will be seen in the following explanation, the methods of assessment also facilitate the students' development in "interdisciplinary study." This is achieved by requiring students to integrate three types of knowledge, role-specific, organizational, and of the self, in the analysis of their learning experience at work.

Many undergraduate students in HEIs today have considerable experience of the workplace prior to entering higher education and indeed, may be spend significant amount of their time as an employee whilst studying. Similarly, they may be engaged in voluntary work or have domestic responsibilities alongside their role as a student. However, for most students, the concept of the workplace as a place where knowledge is generated and which has its own "curriculum" (Major, 2002, 2005) is new. Therefore, a pedagogy for work-based learning needs to provide ways of making students aware of these possibilities, and to develop their skills to recognise, capture, and critique this knowledge. The pedagogy discussed in this chapter achieves this through the development of three areas of self-development: learning how learning takes place; critical reflection on personal learning; and the recognition and development of capabilities (see Figure 8.1).

Whilst the focus appears to be on the student's individual learning, as a result of students' engagement with their workplace through their assessment tasks, opportunities are provided for "organizational learning" to take place within the workplace, particularly where students have been set a particular project to undertake for the employer.

In order for students to conceptualize their work-based learning module as different and more intellectually and socially challenging than a period of assessed work experience, a number of activities are undertaken before the placement takes place. Students are introduced to the purpose and organization of the module during their first year of study, through meetings and seminars, and are involved in the selection of their placement during the second year. "Placement fairs" are held where local, national, and international placement providers meet with students to provide more details of the opportunities offered within their organizations. Letters of application and CVs are composed and sent to their chosen employer and job descriptions discussed and generated for their placement role. These "employment-seeking" tasks often require students to approach this experience in a more professional manner than that which they have been accustomed to with part-time employment. The activities also introduce students to the importance of being able to recognize the behavioral signals on which workplace culture is based, to practice appropriate styles of communication, including non-verbal communication, and to become familiar with the procedures involved in securing employment from both the employee and the employer's perspective.

Immediately prior to the placement, which takes place during the second half of the final semester of level 2, students attend a compulsory "support

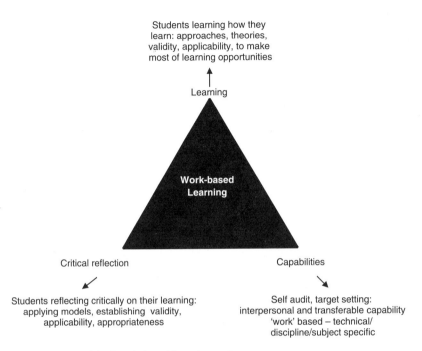

Figure 8.1 A model of work-based learning pedagogy.

Source: Brodie and Irving, 2007.

program" where the philosophy and aims of the module are discussed, together with detailed preparation for the assessment tasks. Students identify and negotiate personal learning outcomes for their placement, as well as learning how to demonstrate previously established learning outcomes relating to the demonstration of knowledge about the aims, objectives, and broader operating context of their placement's organization.

Giving ownership to students for creating their own learning outcomes is a valuable, if challenging, activity. For many, this is the first time that they have considered the concept of a "learning outcome" in detail and of how learning outcomes need to be constructively aligned with their assessment. Similarly, the learning that students need to plan in order to understand the cultural and organizational background to their placement (through activities such as designing a "cultural web" and undertaking analyses in a PESTEL—Political, Economic, Social, Technical, Environmental and Legislative—framework) takes most students into new discipline areas: social psychology, economics and law, whilst reinforcing and applying knowledge for those for whom these concepts are familiar. For all students, uncovering the knowledge about how an organization really works is a journey of enlightenment, particularly when they recognize that the espoused organizational aims and values are not always those demonstrated through the experience of employees and other stakeholders, and that however well-planned an organisation is internally, external factors often have a major effect on how work is conducted and controlled. In common with other interdisciplinary learning situations, this process of recognizing "how the world works" (or "how the subject knowledge is constructed") requires students to learn how other knowledge bases are developed, structured, and informed, and to appreciate why this may be so. A practical example of this new understanding might be, for example, that a student develops their understanding of the basis of the legal system and how it influences working life, or within a specific job role, of the science underpinning industrial processes. Fostering the ability to stand back and critique knowledge in these areas is an important part of the learning process too and links, as will be shown later, to how students' skills of critical reflection are developed, applied, and demonstrated in assessment activities.

Exploring approaches to identifying students' own learning needs and preferences, linked to aspirations for the work placement and to longer-term academic and career-planning goals (for example, potential projects for undergraduate dissertations, postgraduate study, or experience prior to entering professional training on graduation) is valuable for students. Again, new self-insights may be achieved by engaging with (and importantly, critiquing) approaches to identifying, for example, one's own team-working skills, and the circumstances and design of both favorable and less constructive learning experiences from the past. In setting their own learning outcomes for skills and knowledge, students are required to analyze not only learning to date but also to conceptualize how they will plan and negotiate new learning opportunities in a work-based setting.

Prior to going on placement, of course, work-based learning students design their learning outcomes from a theoretical perspective: they cannot be sure until the experience is complete whether they will capture the organizational knowledge and achieve the learning-outcomes that they planned. In order to help clarify the students' aims, to provide an opportunity for others to critique their approach, and to develop presentation and organizational skills, the first part of the assessment for the module is undertaken at the end of the support program. This requires students to give a short presentation to an audience of peers and to answer questions which focus on their aspirations for their placement, their planned learning outcomes, and their approaches to achieving them.

Both the discussion and the plans to achieve learning outcomes are assessed through this presentation, contributing in part to all three cornerstones of the pedagogical approach: learning how to learn, critical reflection, and developing capability. However, it is not until the student engages in the workplace that these three aspects of the pedagogy are fully applied and their potential fully utilized. For learning to be recognized during their work placement, students need to employ the process of critical reflection, in order to analyze their personal learning process.

The process of reflection is integral to many approaches to professional development. Consequently, its use has been critiqued in the research literature in this area by those who recognize that unless it is rigorosly undertaken its benefits may be limited. For example, Clouder (2000) has considered the importance of engaging in reflective critical dialogue about the achievement of learning in health practice settings as well as through reflective writing. To validate learning claims, critical reflection needs to incorporate processes for establishing the truth of what has been learnt and why. Preferably, the model will also include a "spiral" element, using the recognized learning to set future challenges and objectives, thus enabling transformational and sustainable learning to take place. This latter attribute, when related to the assessment of learning, is particularly important in the development of students' skills for lifelong learning, as Boud (2000) has discussed.

In order to develop the skills of critical reflection, students are required to keep a "reflective learning log" during their placement. They are presented with various models of reflection, modified where necessary to embrace the critical aspects of reflection, that is, how evidence external to the situation, such as external sources of information, experience, and theory, inform the final conclusions and learning gained from the experience. The second element of the module's assessment consists of a written report presented shortly after the placement has been completed, presenting both learning about the organization and a critique of how personal learning outcomes have been achieved.

Returning to the concept of interdisciplinary study and the impact of this particular work-based learning experience on student abilities, we need to consider the pedagogy employed and learning outcomes achieved from the perspective of knowledge integration and, it is argued here, its potential for enriching future learning. Clearly, students will vary according to the nature of their work experience and the divergence it presents from their existing knowledge base within undergraduate study. Similarly, if students are already studying on joint honors programs (that, at this HEI, are not restricted to combinations of subjects within particular faculties), they may already have had exposure to different epistemological approaches and traditions of research from which new knowledge is developed. However, it is perhaps the learning and teaching for the holistic nature of the assessment that provides the greatest potential for developing skills for interdisciplinary study. Questioning the validity of claims for knowledge and learning in the complex work setting not only provides a critical base for self-development and organizational development but also intellectual skills for recognizing and appreciating the nature of knowledge creation in both similar and disparate disciplines and in the context of life-long learning.

References

Boud, D. (2000). Sustainable assessment: Rethinking assessment for the learning society. *Studies in Continuing Education, 22*(2), 151–167.
Boud, D., and Solomon, N. (Eds.) (2001). *Work-based learning: A new higher education.* Buckingham: Open University Press.
Brennan, J., and Little, B. (2006). *Towards a strategy for workplace learning.* London: Centre for Higher Education Research and Information/KPMG Consultants.
Brodie, P., and Irving, K. (2007). Assessment in work-based learning: Investigating a pedagogical approach to enhance student learning. *Assessment and Evaluation in Higher Education, 32*(1), 11–19.
Major, D. (2002). The place and status of knowledge in work based learning. In *Conference proceedings. Work Based Learning Network of the Universities Association for Continuing Education.* Cardiff: University of Wales Institute.
Major, D. (2005). Learning through work-based learning. In P. Hartley, A. Woods, and M. Pill, (Eds.), *Enhancing teaching in higher education: new approaches for improving student learning.* London: Routledge.
Shearer, M. C. (2007). Implementing a new interdisciplinary model: The challenges and the benefits of working across disciplines. *Practice and Evidence of Scholarship of Teaching and Learning in Higher Education, 2*(1), 2–20. Retrived May 19, 2007, from http://www.pestlhe.org.uk/index.php/pestlhe/article/viewFile/24/115.

9

Student Feedback on Interdisciplinary Programs

LEE HARVEY

The Higher Education Academy, York

As student feedback in the U.K. shifts into its fourth phase it is noticeable how little attention has been paid to the collection and analysis of views of students on interdisciplinary, cross-disciplinary, or combined studies courses.

The first phase, up to the 1990s, saw little or no formal feedback mechanisms designed to obtain student views in higher education institutions. Where student feedback impacted on the student experience it came, usually, as a result of direct conversations, or even action, on the part of individuals or groups of students. In the pre-mass higher education, this *ad hoc* engagement worked up to a point but did not engender a sense of student-centeredness or responsibility, on the part of the teacher, to address concerns of the students. The latter had to sink or swim in the system as it was.

The 1990s saw the flourishing of formal student feedback, overwhelmingly through the medium of questionnaires. Much data was collected, some of it was analyzed, little of it was reported back to students, and very little of it resulted in any meaningful action. Change that occurred tended to bypass questionnaires and was the result of direct feedback, via conversations over coffee or in corridors, in course committees, or by dint of students voting with their feet. The main reasons for the relative impotence of the feedback in phase two was that questions were framed from the point of view of the teacher (or worse, manager), often limited to a standardized set of module-based items relating to teacher performance. These failed to address student learning, failed to address student concerns, and became tokenistic accountability rituals, the outcomes of which were usually deemed confidential and thus inaccessible. At root, the impotence was compounded by an entire lack of structure designed to act upon the results. Data was collected and mostly shelved; eventually it became obvious to all concerned that the ritual was alienating students and becoming counterproductive.

The third phase, which continues today, overlapped the second and saw some pioneering institutions start to develop a structured mechanism for dealing with, not simply collecting, student feedback. Lines of responsibility for action were developed with appropriate, although not bureaucratically burdensome, reporting and sanctions. In the main, these developments operated at the level of whole institutional feedback surveys: student satisfaction surveys that acted as a barometer of the total student experience. In some places, the development of these centrally run surveys was also co-ordinated with locally (unit or module) owned surveys of teacher capability and with service departments, own "customer" feedback. However, this continues to be a logistical and organizational problem for larger institutions. Alongside this tendency to develop total student experience surveys, some institutions stuck to module-level data collection but developed a more co-ordinated approach to acting on the outcomes. However, this is still relatively rare and an assumption remains prevalent that instituting an institution-wide module survey, asking everyone the same set of questions, constitutes a co-ordinated approach. The key to any student feedback is not the collection of data but the creation of a mechanism for using it to implement improvements.

The fourth phase, which is upon us in the U.K., undermines the concerted improvement approach of the third phase. The National Student Survey, with its trivial set of questions, not only takes us back to phase two but shifts the emphasis from internal quality improvement to external profile, from substance to image and from clearly useful data to superficial indicators designed for spurious comparative purposes rather than as valuable management information. As the struggle for student feedback unfolds, the concerns of interdisciplinary students continues to be ignored.

Students on non-standard programs are usually perceived as a problem when it comes to collecting their views, analyzing, and reporting them. They do not, of course, fit standard categories: they have to be slotted into categories of their own and generally make the whole reporting messy. However, the tendency to bulge out of pre-set categories is but the least of the issues. Much more important is that the views expressed by interdisciplinary students are frequently ignored because it is not clear who is responsible for doing anything about them. Even worse, no one asks questions, in the first place, that are germane to interdisciplinary students. Student feedback questionnaires, explored below in more detail, tend towards a generic set of issues that are premised on the single subject model.

Student Feedback Processes

Most higher education institutions, around the world, collect some type of feedback from students about their experience of higher education, particularly the service they receive. This may include perceptions about the learning and teaching, the learning support facilities (such as libraries and computing facilities), the learning environment, (lecture rooms, laboratories, social space, and university buildings), support facilities (refectories, student accommodation, health facilities, student services) and external aspects of being a student (such as finance and transport infrastructure).

Student views are usually collected in the form of "satisfaction" feedback. Sometimes there are attempts to obtain student views on how to improve specific aspects of provision or on their views about potential or intended future developments but this is less usual. Indeed, it is not always clear how views collected from students fit into institutional quality improvement policies and processes. To be effective in quality improvement, data collected from surveys and peer reviews needs to be transformed into information that can be used within an institution to effect change. Experience going back to the late 1980s shows that to make an effective contribution to internal improvement processes, views of students need to be integrated into a regular and continuous cycle of analysis, reporting, action, and feedback.

In many cases it is not always clear that there is a means to close the loop between data collection and effective action, let alone feedback to students on action taken. For this to happen, the institution must have in place a system for:

- Identifying and delegating responsibility for action;
- Encouraging ownership of plans of action;
- Accountability for action taken or not taken;
- Feedback to generators of the data;
- Committing appropriate resources.

Establishing this is not an easy task, which is why so much data on student views is not used to effect change, irrespective of the good intentions of those who initiate the enquiries. It is, thus, more important to ensure an appropriate action cycle than it is to have in place mechanisms for collecting data.

External Information

In an era where there is an enormous choice available to potential students the views of current students offer a useful information resource. Yet very few institutions make the outcomes of student feedback available externally. The University of Central England (UCE), Sheffield Hallam, and a few other institutions are unusual in publishing their institution-wide student feedback survey (which reports to the level of faculty and major programs). The results are available on a public web site as well as published as hard copy with an ISBN number, which has been the case, at UCE, since its inception in the late 1980s.

The National Student Survey (NSS) will provide information but unfortunately the wrong information presented in the wrong way. In comparison with the sophisticated and relevant analyses of institutional student surveys, the NSS items are trivial, imposed irrespective of relevance, designed for comparative purposes based on standardized subject codes, and provide no sensible information on what is necessary to improve the situation. It operates at a distance from the very feedback and action cycles so important in ensuring effective outcomes and, of course, totally ignores the situation of inter-disciplinary students.

Types

Feedback can take various forms, including formal classroom discussions, informal discussions over coffee, facilitated focus groups, web discussion boards, and course committees, as well as the invidious questionnaire. While all the above-mentioned forms of feedback operate in most settings, they tend to attract less official weight than the formal survey of student views; although, ironically, in most cases change is more likely to occur as a result of direct discussion than from the analysis of questionnaire responses. The latter, in many cases, serves only to legitimate the status quo.

We are, however, in an era of student feedback surveys and, if handled appropriately, they can be effective given the appropriate support infra-structure. There are, broadly speaking, five forms:

- Institution-level satisfaction with the total student experience or a specified sub-set of that experience;
- Faculty-level satisfaction with provision;
- Program-level satisfaction with the learning and teaching and related aspects of a particular program of study (for example, BA Business Studies);[1]
- Module-level feedback on the operation of a specific module or unit of study (for example, Introduction to Statistics);
- Teacher-appraisal by students.

Institution-Level Satisfaction

Systematic, institution-wide student feedback about the quality of their total educational experience is an area of growing activity. Such surveys are almost always based on questionnaires, which mainly consist of questions with pre-coded answers augmented by one or two open questions. In the main, these institution-wide surveys are undertaken by a dedicated unit (either internal or external) with expertise in undertaking surveys and producing results to schedule.

Institution-wide surveys tend to encompass most of the services provided by the university and are not to be confused with standardized institutional forms seeking feedback at the program or module level (discussed below). In the main, institution-wide surveys seek to collect data that provide:

- Management information designed to encourage action for improve-ment;
- A descriptive overview of student opinion, which can be reported as part of appropriate accountability procedures.

The derivation of questions used in institution-wide surveys varies. The Student Satisfaction Approach developed at UCE and adopted at Sheffield Hallam, UEL, Oxford Brookes, Buckingham Chilterns University College among others, uses student-determined questions, usually via focus groups. In other institutions, management or committees decide on the questions. Sometimes, institutions use or adapt questionnaires developed at other institutions. It is, though, very important to include the student voice in the determination of questions. This is particularly the case if one wants to capture and include the concerns of interdisciplinary students. It is, therefore, vital to include at least one interdisciplinary student focus group.

The way the results are used also varies. In some cases there is a clear reporting and action mechanism. In others, it is unclear how the data helps inform decisions. In some cases the process has the direct involvement of the senior management, while in other universities action is realized through the committee structure. Again, there is a danger of interdisciplinary students falling down the cracks. Reporting of views of students who do not fall into simple subject groupings often results in their views being sidelined or ignored altogether. Even when they are reported, it is not always clear who is then responsible for taking up the concerns of such students. This compounds the problem of a general lack of questions specific to the interdisciplinary experience—not least the issues of interconnectedness, progression, and coherence.

Feedback to students of outcomes of surveys is an important element of institution-wide surveys but is not always carried out effectively, nor always produces the awareness intended. Some institutions utilize current lines of communication between tutors and students or through the student unions and student representatives. All of these forms depend upon the effectiveness of these lines of communication, which as interdisciplinary students will be aware are strewn with hazards. Other forms of feedback used include: articles in university magazines, posters, and producing summaries aimed at students but these tend to be very generalized and liable to focus on the spectacular and newsworthy rather than the local but important concerns of specific student groups.

Good practice in institutional surveys suggests that if the improvement function is to be effective it is first necessary to establish an action cycle that clearly identifies lines of responsibility and feedback. Furthermore, surveys need to be tailored to fit the improvement needs of the institution. Making use of stakeholder inputs (especially those of students) in the design of questionnaires is a useful process in making the survey relevant. Importance as well as satisfaction ratings are recommended as this provides key indicators of what students regard as crucial in their experience and thus enables a clear action focus.

Faculty-Level Satisfaction with Provision

Faculty-level surveys (based on pre-coded questionnaires) are similar to those undertaken at institution level. They tend to focus only on those aspects of the experience that the faculty controls or can directly influence. They often tend to be an unsatisfactory combination of general satisfaction with facilities and an attempt to gather information on satisfaction with specific learning situations.

In most cases, these surveys are an additional task for faculty administrators, they are often based on an idiosyncratic set of questions, and tend not to be well analyzed, if at all. They are rarely linked into a meaningful improvement action cycle.

Where there is an institution-wide survey, disaggregated and reported to faculty level, faculty-based surveys tend to be redundant. Where faculty surveys overlap with institutional ones, there is often dissonance that affects response rates. If faculty-level surveys are undertaken they should not clash with institution-wide surveys, where both coexist; it is probably better to attempt to collect faculty data through qualitative means, focusing on faculty-specific issues untouched by institution-wide surveys.

If faculty-level surveys are undertaken they must be properly analyzed and linked into a faculty-level action and feedback cycle, otherwise cynicism will rapidly manifest itself and undermine the credibility of the whole process.

Program-Level Satisfaction with the Learning and Teaching

Program-level surveys are not always based on questionnaires although most tend to be. In some cases, feedback on programs is solicited through qualitative discussion sessions, which are minuted. These may make use of focus groups. Informal feedback on programs is a continuous part of the dialogue between students and lecturers. This should not be overlooked as it is an important source of information for improvement at this level.

Program-level surveys tend to focus on the teaching and learning, course organization, and program-specific learning resources. However, in a modularized environment, program-level analysis of the learning situation tends to be "averaged" and does not necessarily provide clear indicators of potential improvement of the program without further enquiry at the module level.

The link into any action is far from apparent in many cases. Where a faculty undertakes a survey of all its programs of this type, there may be mechanisms, in theory, to encourage action but, in practice, the time lag involved in processing the questionnaires by hard-pressed faculty administrators tends to result in little timely improvement following the feedback.

In a modularized environment, where modular-level feedback is encouraged (see below), there is less need for program-level questionnaire surveys. Where the institution-wide survey is comprehensive and disaggregates to the level of programs, there is also a degree of redundancy in program-level surveys. Again, if program-level and institutional-level run in parallel there is a danger of dissonance. Program-level questionnaire surveys are probably not necessary if the institution has both a well-structured institution-wide survey, reporting to program level, and structured module-level feedback. However, if there are interdisciplinary programs, specific program feedback could be an effective way of complementing more generic survey results.

If specific program-level information is needed for improvement purposes, it is probably better to obtain qualitative feedback on particular issues through discussion sessions or focus groups. If program-level surveys are undertaken they must be properly analyzed and linked into a program-level action and feedback cycle. This tends to be a rarity in most institutions.

Module-Level Feedback

Feedback on specific modules or units of study provide an important element of continuous improvement. The feedback tends to focus on the specific learning and teaching associated with the module, along with some indication of the problems of accessing module-specific learning resources. Module-level feedback, both formal and informal, involves direct or mediated feedback from students to teachers about the learning situation within the module or unit of study.

The primary form of feedback at this level is direct informal feedback via dialogue. However, although this feedback may often be acted upon it is rarely evident in any accounts of improvements based on student feedback.

In most institutions, there is a requirement for some type of formal collection and reporting of module-level feedback, usually to be included in program annual reports. In the main, institutions do not specify a particular data collection process. The lecturer(s) decide on the appropriate method for the formal collection of feedback. Often, though, institutions provide guidance and formal questionnaire templates, should the module leader(s) wish to use them.

There is a tendency to use "feedback questionnaires" at this level: sometimes standardized questionnaires across the institution, sometimes faculty-wide, and sometimes constructed locally. Module-level questionnaire feedback is usually superficial, results in little information on what would improve the learning situation and, because of questionnaire-processing delays, rarely benefits the students who provide the feedback. The use of questionnaires tends to inhibit qualitative discussion at the unit level.

Direct, qualitative feedback is far more useful in improving the learning situation within a module of study. Qualitative discussion between staff (or facilitators) and students about the content and approach in particular course units or modules provides a rapid and in-depth appreciation of positive and negative aspects of taught modules. Direct feedback may take the form of an open, formally minuted discussion between students and teacher(s), informal feedback over coffee, or a focus-group session, possibly facilitated by an independent outsider. If written feedback is required, open questions are used that encourage students to say what would constitute an improvement for them, rather than rating items on a schedule drawn up by a teacher or, worse, an administrator.

However, qualitative feedback is sometimes seen as more time-consuming to arrange and analyze and, therefore, as constituting a less popular choice than handing out questionnaires. Where compliance overshadows motivated improvement, recourse to questionnaires is likely.

In many instances, questionnaires used for module-level feedback are not analyzed properly or in a timely fashion. Although most institutions insist on the collection of module-level data, the full cycle of analysis, reporting, action, and feedback to originators of the data rarely occurs. There is, of course, considerable potential, at module level, of exploring issues pertinent to interdisciplinary students. However, this requires an imaginative and creative approach. Using standardized questionnaires is unlikely to be much use as they will probably not include relevant questions. For interdisciplinary students, the open-ended questions that are often appended to module tick-box surveys are likely to be most useful. Indeed, it might be argued that, in general, this is the most useful feature of module feedback, although sadly under-analyzed in many cases.

Module-level feedback is vital for the ongoing evolution of modules and the teaching team needs to be responsive to both formal and informal feedback. Both formal and informal feedback should be included when reporting at the module-level. Module-level feedback is necessary to complement institution-wide surveys, which cannot realistically report to module-level. Module-level feedback should be tailored to the improvement and development needs of the module. There is no need for standardized, institution-wide, module-level questionnaires. Making comparisons between modules is trivial and far less effective than year-on-year monitoring of trends in student views about the module. As with any other feedback, module-level feedback of all types must be properly analyzed and linked into a module-level action and feedback cycle.

Appraisal of Teacher Performance by Students

As a result of government pressure in the 1990s, institutions went through a period of collecting student views on the performance of particular teachers, known as "teacher assessment." Many institutions use standardized program- or module-based surveys of student appraisal of teaching. The use of student evaluations of teacher performance are sometimes part of a broader peer- and self-assessment approach to teaching quality. In some cases, they are used as part of the individual review of staff and can be taken into account in promotion and tenure situations (although this is, as yet, rare in the U.K.).

Teacher-appraisal surveys may provide some inter-program comparison of teacher performance. However, standardized teacher-appraisal questionnaires tend, in practice, to focus on a limited range of areas and rarely address the development of student learning. Often, the standardized form is a bland compromise, designed by managers or a committee, which serves nobody's purposes. They are often referred to by the derogatory label of "happy forms" as they are usually a set of questions about the reliability, enthusiasm, knowledge, encouragement, and communication skills of named lecturers.

Student appraisal of teachers tends to be a blunt instrument. Depending on the questions and the analysis it has the potential to identify very poor teaching but, in the main, the results give little indication of how things can be improved. Appraisal forms are rarely of much use for incremental and continuous improvement.

In the vast majority of cases, there is no feedback at all to students about outcomes. The views on individual teacher performance are usually deemed confidential and subject to closed performance-review or development interviews with a senior manager. Copenhagen Business School is a rare example of an institution that, in the 1990s, published the results within the institution.

Students' appraisal of teacher performance has a limited function, which, in practice, is ritualistic rather than improvement-oriented. Any severe problems are usually identified quickly via this mechanism. Repeated use leads to annoyance and cynicism on the part of students and teachers. Students become disenchanted because they rarely receive any feedback on the views they have offered. Lecturers become cynical and annoyed because they see student appraisal of teaching as a controlling rather than improvement-oriented tool.

Good practice suggests that surveys of student appraisal of teaching should be used sparingly, without continually repeating the process. It also helps to ask about the student learning as well as the teacher performance. Ensuring that action is taken, and seen to be taken, to resolve and monitor the problems that such appraisals identify is important. However, this focus is usually not helpful in exploring the subtleties of student learning issues, such as those experienced by interdisciplinary students.

Multiple Surveys: Cosmetic or Inclusive

Institutions often have a mixture of the different type of student feedback, to which might be added graduate and employer surveys. The information gathered is, far too often, simply that—information. There are many circumstances when nothing is done with the information. It is not used to effect changes. Often it is not even collected with a use in mind. Perhaps, far too often, it is a cosmetic exercise.

There is more to student feedback than collecting data. In general:

- If collecting student views only collect what can be made use of.

- It is counterproductive to ask students for information then not use it; students become cynical and uncooperative if they think no one really cares about what they think.
- It is important to heed, examine, and make use of student views.
- If data from surveys of students is going to be useful then it needs to be transformed into meaningful information.
- The information needs to be clearly reported, fed into systems of accountability, and linked to a process of continuous quality improvement: the whole process must be accountable and part of a culture of improvement.
- It is important to ensure that action takes place on the basis of student views and that action is seen to take place.
- This requires clear lines of communication, so that the impact of student views are fed back to students: in short, there needs to be a line of accountability back to the students to close the circle; it is not sufficient that students find out indirectly, if at all, that they have had a role in institutional policy.
- Data from different sources needs to be co-ordinated and triangulated.

Students are important stakeholders in the quality-monitoring and assessment processes and it is useful to obtain their views. In doing so, it is important not to inadvertently sideline the views of specific groups, of which interdisciplinary students are a group often rendered invisible.

Significant Differences

There is, as was noted at the start of this chapter, little research on the differences in perspectives between interdisciplinary and single-subject students. Despite all the surveying, reported results ignore this dimension in most cases and thus hard evidence of differences in perception is in short supply.

One London university that undertook an institution-wide survey in 2004 separated out the responses of 90 combined honors students. Their views, on issues designed for all students, were very similar to the university average on most of the 100 or so items. The areas where they diverged hint at some underlying issues that might be germane to any collection of interdisciplinary student views. Results were reported on an A to E scale (very satisfactory (A) to very unsatisfactory (E)) with very important items represented in upper case and less important ones in lower case.

- Availability (b) and support from course representatives (c) were less important than for the university overall (B and C respectively).
- Promptness of feedback on assignments was more satisfactory (B) than for the university overall (C).
- Development of analytical (A) and of critical skills (A) were more satisfactory compared to the university overall (B in both cases).

- Aspects of a course that prepares you for employment was less satisfactory (C) compared to the university mean (B).
- Opportunities to go on work experience (D) and opportunities to network with professionals (D) were both unsatisfactory compared to adequate (C) for the university overall.
- The extent to which classes run as scheduled was very satisfactory (A) compared to the university mean (B).
- Availability of personal tutors (C), support from personal tutors (C), and ready access to academic and pastoral advice (C) were less satisfactory than for the university as a whole (B for all three items).
- Combined honors students were much more regular users of the learning resource centre than most other groups of students. However, these students were marginally less satisfied with the facility than students on average. They were less satisfied with the range of books (C) and multiple copies of core books (D) and with noise levels (C), compared with university averages (of B, C, and B respectively).
- Combined honors students were also more satisfied with opening hours of the computer rooms (A) and reliability of computers (B) than the university mean (B and C, respectively).
- Combined honors students were less satisfied with procedures for enrolment (C) than their peers (B).

Combined honors students' overall ratings showed a more positive view of the university as a whole (66.1%), higher than students from other schools and considerably above the mean (62.9%) for the university overall. Their rating for their course (69.3%) was above the mean (67.7) but eclipsed by the means in five of the nine other schools. However, they rated their potential career prospects poorly (62.7%) compared to the university mean of (64.9%). Asked whether they would still choose their course, respondents were positive (5.0 on a 7-point scale) but below the university mean of 5.3.

Another university, in the north, reported the results for a small group of combined honors students separately in 2002.

- Opportunities for work-related placements (d) and quality of workplace experience (c) were less satisfactory (but less important) than for the university as a whole (B in both cases). Similarly, there was less satisfaction with "the course prepares you for the work place" (C compared to the university mean of B).
- Ease with which teaching staff could be contacted (B) is slightly less satisfactory than the university mean (A). However, they are more satisfied (B) than any other groups (B) with the manageability of their workload. They also regard the opportunity to present work to peers/staff as more important than other groups of students.
- They are more satisfied with noise levels (A) and availability of quiet

work space in the learning centre than the university mean (B in both cases).

- They are also more satisfied with the range of media materials (A compared to B for the university as a whole).
- Combined studies students regarded the efficiency of the enrolment procedure (B) and induction to the university (B) as more important than students on average (b and b) and were more satisfied with notification of timetable/room alterations (B compared to C).
- They were slightly less satisfied with the range of software available (B compared to A) but more satisfied with the helpfulness of technical support staff (A compared to B).
- Combined studies students were alone in being dissatisfied with the value for money of their course (D) (compared to other schools).

These two sets of independent results hint at some issues for combined studies students around workplace learning and belonging. There is a suggestion that they are to some extent better served administratively but that they are less satisfied with central learning support, partly because they spend a lot of time using it. Much more needs to be done to explore these initial limited results.

Note

1. In some institutions programs of study are referred to as "courses" or "pathways." However, "course" is a term used in some institutions to mean "module" or "unit" of study, that is, a sub-element of a program of study. Due to the ambiguity of "course," the terms "program of study" and "module" are used in this chapter.

II
Vertical
*Matters that Apply
to a Field of Study*

10
Interdisciplinary Tourism Education

TAZIM JAMAL AND DAWN JOURDAN
Texas A&M University

Introduction

The wide-ranging scale and scope of tourism make it a very difficult and complex phenomenon to define and study. Leiper (1979), using a systems approach, defines tourism in terms of five key elements: tourists, transit routes, generating regions, destination regions, and a tourism industry. It involves individuals, groups, and societies in relation with built-physical-ecological spaces and structures. Thus, its impacts are far-reaching, extending from the local to the global. In keeping with the complexity of this phenomenon, tourism studies has evolved as a kaleidoscope of fields or specializations arising within key disciplinary settings such as economics, business management, sociology, psychology, geography, and anthropology (Jafari and Ritchie, 1981). It is therefore useful for the purpose of this chapter to distinguish between four aspects of tourism: tourism as a phenomenon, tourism as a field of study (research and developing a body of knowledge), tourism education (training and pedagogy), plus tourism as professional/industry practice. Our focus here is primarily on tourism pedagogy, particularly cross-disciplinary issues in sustainable tourism education.

The global initiative on sustainable development (WCED, 1987) has produced a growing discourse of "sustainable tourism." This holistic development paradigm attempts to integrate ecological, social, cultural, economic, and political systems to ensure the well-being of present and future generations (Bramwell et al., 1996; Holden, 2000; UNEP-ICLEI, 2003). The overall sustainability paradigm is also cross-disciplinary, and requires a range of skills, knowledge, and tools. Planning for sustainable tourism, as shown in Table 10.1, requires (i) theoretical understanding of local-global sustainability issues, (ii) technical knowledge to develop and apply tools for sustainable development and planning, and (iii) practical knowledge to make informed decisions on the trade-offs required to attain individual, societal and ecological good (through "sustainable tourism" practices).

As sustainability issues become more pressing in the twenty-first century, the development of multidisciplinary or interdisciplinary tourism curricula and degree-granting programs takes on even greater importance. Such

Table 10.1 Components of planning for sustainable tourism

Research interest	Theoretical (Episteme)	Technical (Techne)	Practical (Phronesis)	Critical praxis
Research paradigm	(Post) positivistic in the physical/biological sciences; may be social constructionist within some social science and liberal studies	(Post) positivistic	Interpretive	Critical research
Main disciplinary or study locus	Theoretical and empirical-analytical sciences	Empirical analytical sciences	Hermeneutic sciences	Critical theory, poststructural, postcolonial, feminist, cultural and Marxist studies
Concern	"Discovery" of knowledge; universals and knowledge production that is invariable in time and space (Flyvbjerg, 2001)	Measurement, explanation and prediction; efficient use of resources; tourism system complexities, impact management	Experience, meaning and understanding	Excluded voices; lack of participatory democracy; capitalist exploitation of natural + cultural "resources"
Focus	Standpoint and foundational epistemologies theoretical *know why*	Systems modeling, variables, planning, indicators, causality, certainty; technical *know how*	Perceptions, values and beliefs, interpretations; phronesis (prudence, or practical common-sense: Flyvbjerg, 2001)	Justice, disciplinary practices, domination, language, identity, resistance, contingency; praxis
Desired outcomes	Theoretical paradigms and solutions	Control, management, reduction of uncertainty; sustainable development, ecological modernization	Inclusion of traditional and local knowledge, practical knowledge, experience and insights	Intervention, change, self-direction, emancipation, inclusion of marginalized interests
Curriculum, research approach and instruction	Theoretical research (in-house), theory-driven syllabi, assignments and examinations. Neutral instructor imparting objective knowledge	Case studies; apprenticeships; course-based field study; focus on technical skill development (e.g. planning, economic impact assessments, etc.). Technically proficient instructor	Case studies, role play, internship programs; field studies. Qualitative (interpretive) research. Instructor as facilitator of dialogue/learning	Case studies, role play, field studies with direct participation in projects. Participatory/action research, critical interpretive research. Instructor also directly involved in coordinating critical insights and facilitating critical practice (praxis)

cross-disciplinarity involves developing close relationships between various functions (like marketing, accounting, operations management, finance), and between disciplines, e.g., geography, psychology, sociology, anthropology, management, architecture/planning (Jafari and Ritchie, 1981; Leiper, 2000; Prezclawski, 1993). Significant challenges thus arise with respect to the types of knowledge and skills required by tourism scholars and practitioners, and the types of education and training programs required to articulate, develop and implement an integrated framework for sustainable tourism.

These are the interdisciplinary considerations and concepts which need to be applied in the development of sustainable tourism:

- Definition/description of ST (Bramwell et al., 1996); general (global) and local principles reflecting sustainability approach (World Commission on Environment and Development, WCED 1987).
- Philosophical/theoretical development of terms and concepts related to definition, principles, codes of ethics, equity and economic/environmental/social justice, etc.
- Methodological considerations; various theoretical paradigms and methods; adapting techniques and constructs such as "carrying capacity to suit social context of tourism destinations, hence the evolution of concepts such as 'limits of acceptable change.' " Cultural studies and studies of change (anthropological, geographical, critical).
- Sociology of tourism and tourism psychology (motivation, well-being, leisure and society).
- Approaches to ecosystems management, operations management, impact assessment and feasibility studies that are holistic, i.e., consider economic, social, cultural, environmental and political impacts jointly; sustainability indicators, full-cost accounting; systems-based approaches.
- Strategic tourism planning—based on ST principles; address process and content aspects; include urban and landscape design, park planning, comprehensive planning, marketing planning, implementing, and monitoring (Hall and Lew 1999; Holden, 2000).
- Historic preservation and heritage management—integrate ecological, cultural and historic preservation aspects; address cultural critique of "heritage" and implications for heritage tourism.

Our chapter examines the challenge of creating a cross-disciplinary curriculum to meet the needs of those who operate in the field of sustainable tourism and those acting from other disciplines in tourism-related fields. We commence by presenting two contested conceptual frameworks in the next section: interdisciplinary and multidisciplinary curricula. We illustrate and discuss these using practical examples from our own graduate university curricula at Texas A&M University (College Station, U.S.), in (i) Recreation, Park, and

Tourism Sciences (RPTS), (ii) Architecture and Planning, and (iii) Historic Preservation. These were chosen because they are necessary cross-disciplinary linkages for students pursuing education in sustainable tourism and other related fields. Further, these academic programs contain certificate programs and courses that embrace inter- and multidisciplinary approaches. The chapter therefore focuses on the cross-disciplinary challenge of *sustainable tourism pedagogy* at the university level, with a special emphasis on planning and preservation of community and ecological and cultural heritage resources.

Multidisciplinary Programs in Tourism Studies

Conceptual Development

Historically, the study of tourism has evolved as a pastiche of intra-disciplinary fields or areas of concentration, incorporating or developing multidisciplinary perspectives over time. Echtner and Jamal (1997) draw upon Kuhn's (1970) *The Structure of Scientific Revolutions* to argue that tourism as a field of study is in a pre-paradigmatic state, sorting out theoretical frameworks, addressing methodological and philosophical debates, and working through various forms of organization and legitimation (see Flyvberg, 2001). Within geography, for example, Hall and Page (1999) examine the geography of tourism and recreation under three interrelated areas of Grano's (1981) model of external influences and internal change in geography: *knowledge* (substantive content of the study area), *action* (research within the context of research praxis), and *culture* (academics and students within the research community and wider society). Accumulating and legitimizing a body of knowledge (theoretical and methodological paradigms) and practices are crucial activities in a field's evolution, with important implications for cross-disciplinary education in tourism.

According to Jafari (1991, 2001), four distinct research platforms have arisen chronologically (without replacing each other) in the process of tourism emerging as a field of study: the Advocacy, Cautionary, Adaptancy, and the Knowledge-based platform. Commencing with economic and development-related activities and economics (Advocacy), the field progressed to a growing awareness of tourism impacts (Cautionary) and impact management (Adaptancy, e.g., identifying social-cultural impacts and addressing ecological conservation, historic preservation, and more recently, interpretation and cultural heritage). The most recent platform represents a scientific body of knowledge being accumulated over time (the Knowledge-based platform).[1] Further to this, we identified a couple of contestations in relation to this scientific body of knowledge that are important to tourism education and research.

Some scholars argue that "tourism studies" is evolving towards a distinct discipline (Leiper, 1981, 2000), while others claim that tourism curricula should recognize the indiscipline of tourism (Tribe, 1997). This debate is important to the development of cross-disciplinary tourism program. For instance, those who subscribe to the first view will attempt to do more than merely bridge disciplines by drawing upon courses in different departments— they will attempt to create interdisciplinary rather than multidisciplinary tourism programs. Following Leiper (1981), a *multidisciplinary* approach to education enables courses and insights from other disciplines to be used to inform the subject within one's own discipline; this includes applying theories, methods, and other tools that are perceived to be relevant. An *interdisciplinary* approach takes these insights and information, and develops new theoretical paradigms and tools. It can be argued that the development of tourism as a distinct discipline involves interdisciplinarity: "working *between* the disciplines, *blending* various philosophies and techniques, so that the particular disciplines do not stand apart but are brought together intentionally and explicitly to seek a synthesis" (Leiper, 1981, p. 72).

We concur with Echtner and Jamal (1997) that "tourism studies" is in a preparadigmatic stage, and a body of knowledge is slowly beginning to take shape with the emergence of new journals, conferences, tourism study programs, and an international community of scholars. The knowledge-based platform is evolving by drawing upon theories and methods from different disciplines and issues/insights from practice (in the "real" world). Such cross-disciplinary borrowing and adapting are resulting in multidisciplinary and interdisciplinary forms of knowledge. What is less clear is the role of cross-disciplinary tourism education in the development of the knowledge-based platform. The examples below and the discussion in the next section reveal a spectrum of multidisciplinary and interdisciplinary activities and effects in programs related to sustainability and "tourism studies." These present different philosophical and practical challenges to the pedagogy and practice of sustainable tourism as a cross-disciplinary endeavor. Some key activities and issues in multidisciplinary and interdisciplinary tourism education are described and discussed in the following sections.

Multidisciplinary Approaches

In recent years, some universities have begun to recognize the need for the creation of educational programs which build on or borrow from the teachings of other disciplines or the development of specializations within a particular domain. The extent of the scale and scope of issues and impacts in tourism calls for diverse theoretical, technical, and educational tools to enable the "sustainable" development and management of ecological and cultural-heritage spaces of visitation. While some commercial and management-oriented tourism programs are located in business schools, others are situated in cross-disciplinary settings such as the Department of Recreation, Park and Tourism Sciences (RPTS) at Texas A&M University (www.rpts.tamu.edu). Situated within the College of Agriculture, RPTS offers a variety of courses and programs intended to provide a multidisciplinary education in recreation, park, and tourism development and management. New specializations are currently in process, such as conservation and park management (i.e., national parks in addition to traditional focus on urban parks), tourism impacts management, and the development of a certification program in community development.

Curriculum changes also reflect the addition of qualitative methodology course requirements to the mandatory quantitative courses typical of such departments. In part, these new areas have emerged due to a growing acknowledgement of the diverse character and social-cultural impacts of recreation and tourism, and of the sustainability challenges faced by the industry overall. While the RPTS department has not explicitly adopted a sustainability-oriented curriculum, a number of its courses adopt a sustainability-oriented philosophy (e.g., RPTS 426, Tourism Impacts and Planning). Effectiveness remains a problem due to lack of coordination and commitment to the training of sustainability-oriented practitioners and researcher. By contrast, a number of programs have arisen globally that explicitly embrace a sustainability paradigm. Consider, for instance, the post-graduate program in Sustainable Tourism (MSc/certificate/diploma) at Sheffield Hallam University, England, which lists the following topics under "Course Content":

- critical thinking and investigation methods
- tourism policy and planning
- tourism, culture and society
- sustainability development
- applied management project
- destination marketing
- sustainable tourism
- visitor management
- dissertation/thesis

(Retrieved January 10, 2004, from http://www2.shu.ac.uk/prospectus/op_pglookup1.cfm?id_num=LFM064&status=TN.)

Sustainability Across Departments

While working toward the creation of cross-disciplinary degree programs, faculty members in the College of Architecture at Texas A&M University (TAMU) have also embraced this sustainability challenge through the creation of two multidisciplinary certificate programs: historic preservation and sustainable urbanism. In recognition of the interdisciplinary nature of the field, the Dean of TAMU's College of Architecture has challenged his faculty to develop new programs to better meet the divergent need of students enrolled in the college's degree programs (architecture, landscape architecture and urban planning, and construction science), as well as serving the demands of students enrolled in degree programs outside the college. A number of departments within the college are considering ways to create truly interdisciplinary degree programs for future generations of students housed within the college and others from outside the college who demonstrate an interest in multidisciplinary education. However, given the complexity of determining how to administer such a program, college faculty have sought to provide smaller-scale opportunities for college majors and non-majors to engage in multidisciplinary educational pursuits.

The college offers certificate programs in historic preservation and sustainable urbanism. Approved by the college in November 1995, the certificate program in historic preservation is administered by the Historic Resources Imaging Laboratory, one of the college's research centers. The goal of this certificate program is to provide students "the opportunity to develop a body of knowledge . . . to support their career goals" (retrieved January 25, 2005, from http://archone.tamu.edu/hril/certificate.html). This program is self-identified as cross-disciplinary, based on the belief that "historic preservation is a cross-disciplinary field in which practitioners must have mutual respect for others, while building appropriate awareness, understanding, and abilities within a chosen area of expertise" (Ibid.).

The certificate program in sustainable urbanism was developed much more recently. This program is self-identified as "interdisciplinary" and is based, much like the certificate program in historic preservation, out of another of the college's research centers—the Center for Housing and Urban Development (retrieved January 25, 2005, from http://archweb.tamu.edu/SustainableUrbanism/index.html).[2] The primary goal of this certificate program is "to provide students with an understanding of the interrelationship between sustainability, cities, and the environmental design programs" (Ibid.). The program is open to students from any graduate degree program at Texas A&M University.

Both programs are governed by a certificate council. The certificate council is comprised of members of the graduate faculty from the college and elsewhere with special expertise in the relevant area. In both instances, the members of the certificate councils are appointed by the Dean of the College of Architecture to teach and guide students seeking interdisciplinary educational pursuits. The requirements of both certificate programs are highly similar. Both require students to declare their intention to seek a certificate along with the filing of their degree plans. With respect to the certificate program in historic preservation, students seeking the certificate must enroll in a course entitled the Theory and Practice of Preservation, as well as 12 additional hours of coursework with preservation content. Students enrolled in the program are provided with a list of courses deemed to have the necessary requisite preservation content (Table 10.2).

To ensure that the students' experience is truly cross-disciplinary, program parameters dictate that students take at least three hours of coursework outside their major department. By comparison, students enrolled in the certificate

Table 10.2 Course choices for Historic Preservation Certificate Program

ANTH 605 Conservation of Archeological Resources I
ANTH 606 Conservation of Archeological Resources II
ANTH 608 Folk Life and Material Culture
ANTH 645 Cultural Resources Management
ARCH 646 Philosophy and Practice of Preservation
ARCH 647 Recording Historic Buildings
ARCH 648 Preservation Technology
ARCH 649 Advanced History of Building Technology
GEOG 604 Process in Cultural Geography
LDEV 687 Development Analysis and Feasibility I
LDEV 688 Development Analysis and Feasibility II
PLAN 643 Preservation Law
PLAN 689 Special Topics in Heritage Preservation and Planning
RPTS 307 Methods of Environmental Interpretation
RPTS 646 or RPTS 626 Social Impacts of Tourism

program for sustainable urbanism must complete a minimum of 18 hours of coursework from an approved multidisciplinary list of courses (Table 10.3). At least one course must be outside the student's major discipline (retrieved January 25, 2005, from http://archweb.tamu.edu/SustainableUrbanism/requirements.html). Approved Courses outside the College of Architecture include: GEOG 616 (Urban Geography), RPTS 646 (Heritage Tourism), RPTS 626 (Social Impacts of Tourism), SOCI 620 (Human Ecology) (retrieved 1 January, 2005, from http://archweb.tamu.edu/SustainableUrbanism/approved.html). The sustainable urbanism certificate program culminates in the student's participation in a six-hour collaborative studio.

In addition to these coursework requirements, program parameters require that all enrolled students complete "a professional study, thesis, or dissertation with a Sustainable Urbanism focus approved by the Sustainable Urbanism Certificate Council." Program participants are required to seek for their

Table 10.3 Course choices for Sustainable Urbanism Certificate Program

ARCH 624 Theory of Placemaking
ARCH 689 Site Planning
ARCH 646 Historic Preservation
COSC 662 Housing Production
LAND 612 Landscape Architecture Site Development
LAND 661 Visual Quality Analysis
LAND 641 Environmental Planning
LDEV 661 Environment and Development
LDEV 671 Sustainable Development
PLAN 669 Urban Infrastructure Planning
PLAN 689 Sustainable Transportation

research two committee members, including a chair, who have been appointed by the Dean as faculty fellows for the program. Typically one of the committee members must be situated in a department outside the college where the student's degree program is located. Recent student research has brought together committees composed of faculty members from a number of diverse academic backgrounds, all with an interest in issues related to sustainability.

While cross-disciplinarity is highly encouraged with TAMU's College of Architecture, current efforts appear to be, at best, multidisciplinary in nature. Degree programs and course contents are, with limited exception, isolated within each area, rather than transcending or synthesizing new theoretical and methodological approaches. An overhaul of the way in which programs are developed and degrees are awarded within specific departments may be necessary to overcome the limitations of multidisciplinary education and open up possibilities for greater interdisciplinarity in developing a knowledge-based platform for sustainable tourism.

Moving Towards Interdisciplinarity?

A key challenge for educators in sustainable tourism lies in sorting out and integrating relevant knowledge from the multitude of disciplines that inform tourism studies. These range from critical/cultural studies to the applied/technical fields such as planning and urban design (Table 10.1). Drawing upon ST planning, for instance, decisions need to be made about *process*-related knowledge and experience. For example, training collaborative community planners/architects or praxis-oriented (advocacy) planners would require curriculum attention to theory and practice in communicative planning, neighborhood design charrettes and youth involvement processes (Jourdan, 2004). Moreover, differences exist between programs about the role of *praxis*— active change-oriented participation by the researcher/scholar in the field. Disciplinary and institutional differences in the *content-process-praxis* dimensions are reflected both in the courses and programs offered, as well as within the pedagogic mission, which could range from "neutral" fact and skill-based expert training to encouraging praxis-oriented critical scholars and practitioners (Table 10.1).

In addition to process and praxis, the cross-disciplinary curriculum has to determine and provide the *content* matter, i.e., multidisciplinary and/or interdisciplinary expertise. The multidisciplinary expert (ME) would have a strong core training in a main discipline (either from a previous college degree or from the one currently enrolled in), plus a broad cross-section of courses in disciplines that would contribute relevant knowledge and skills to the student's main study area. By contrast, the interdisciplinary expert (IE) aims to develop a rich interdisciplinary perspective from the study program. Both the ME and the IE could have entered the graduate program with a disciplinary background (e.g. college undergraduate degree in biology, architecture, urban planning, economics), or a multidisciplinary background (e.g., an undergraduate degree in "liberal arts," or in "recreation, park, and tourism" studies). Research into cross-disciplinary program outcomes is crucial since it will help evaluate and decide which combination of undergraduate and graduate education might be most effective for sustainable tourism pedagogy and practice.

Within the Department of Recreation, Park, and Tourism Sciences at Texas A&M University, certain courses and actions reflect an emerging awareness of interdisciplinary education and the concrete training of IE scholars and practitioners. In part these needs are primarily pragmatic and driven by structural issues, for instance, the impact of globalization on agricultural enterprises and coastal shrimping communities in Texas (diversification into nature tourism and heritage tourism has been one policy response reflected in various RPTS research, teaching, and outreach initiatives). New directions are being initiated and taken up within student theses or dissertations. The graduate course in Social Impacts of Tourism (RPTS 626), for instance, is primarily theoretical (occasionally wholly applied to local issues), drawing upon sociological perspectives of tourism and modernity (e.g., Franklin, 2000; Wang, 2000). Cases and small term projects (local level) help illustrate more abstract concepts.

Issues of commodification, authenticity, and representation are dealt with in the graduate Heritage Tourism class through readings from a wide range of disciplines (Table 10.5). The Fall (2004) course syllabus for RPTS 646 reflects

Table 10.4 Examples of macro-micro theoretical directions for developing multi- and interdisciplinary tourism education

Macro approaches:	Cultural studies—Mass communication, cultural production, representation, identity and "the other" (Hall, 1997).
	Evolutionary biology/(eco)psychology theories
	Post-colonialism (applicable to micro-level analysis too)
	Representations and discourses of nature
	Post-structuralism and Postmodernism (critique of power and metanarratives)
	Theories of power, ideology and hegemony, critical (social) theory, discursive and relational forms of power. Sociological approaches, e.g., structuration theory (macro-micro), practice theories. See Mowforth and Munt (2003) applying Bourdieu (1977, 1984)
	Tourism, postmodernism and cultural consumption (Urry, 1990)
	Tourism production system (Britton, 1991; Dann 1996).
Micro approaches:	Experience and meaning (hermeneutics, phenomenology, etc.)
	Practice theory, performance theory; performativity, theatre studies (Jamal et al., 2003)
	The politics of authenticity, identity, ethnicity, culture and heritage.
	Ecofeminism and feminist theory

this theoretical cross-disciplinarity as well as the provision of technical and practical skills:

> This course focuses on the cross-disciplinary study of culture and heritage in tourism, at the local, national and international levels of destination and society. In particular, the course will examine issues of representation, identity and image over time and space. Two areas of emphasis in this course are: (1) Theoretical insights into heritage as related to ethnicity, place, community, power, and the global tourism industry, (2) Practical insights and tools from an applied perspective, for the management of heritage sites/attractions, and related heritage resources. Readings and case examples will draw from tourism studies and other areas such as cultural studies, geography, anthropology, environmental studies, sociology, political science and management. (Source, RPTS 646, Course Syllabus, Fall 2004)

Case studies, hands-on term projects, and visits to local communities, festivals, and events, provide practical skills in both the undergraduate and graduate classes. Problem-solving, critical thinking, and case study analysis are an integral part of the both the IE and ME curriculum offering (Table 10.1). Table 10.4 offers a number of disciplinary and area-specific references, theories, and theorists that might enable new developments in IE, for instance, micro-macro synthesis (micro-macro linkages is one approach for addressing how individual and local-level practices and events relate to social and regional to global level practices and events).[3]

Cross-disciplinary course and programmatic participation of students between RPTS, historic preservation and urban planning (e.g., joint graduate class participation on term projects between historic preservation and RPTS 626 (Spring 2005), as well as between urban planning and RPTS 626 (Spring 2003)) indicate an increased awareness of diverse approaches to tourism studies by graduate students. Teaching evaluations for RPTS 626 and 646 courses, where taught with a theoretical focus in previous years, scored over 4.0 on a scale of 1–5 (where the interval 4–5 denotes very good to excellent). Student comments on the evaluations, while not formally acknowledging cross-disciplinary benefits in evaluation, show both appreciation and apprehension at the richness and diversity of disciplinary influences. Informal conversations and class discussions between students from RPTS and the other two areas (historic preservation and urban planning) also indicate that students perceive distinct benefits from having cross-disciplinary participation in their graduate classes. Two lines of study directions and actions have been observed here:

- Students enrolled in other programs within departments (e.g., sociology, urban planning) can take RPTS 426 (Tourism Impacts and Planning), RPTS 626 (Social Impacts of Tourism), or RPTS 646

(Heritage Tourism) as an elective or for credit towards the certificate program (see above). These students generally adopt a ME perspective, and often request the course instructor to be on their graduate advisory committee. Occasionally, such students may choose to co-chair their dissertation program thus supplementing their main study area with a strong bridge with tourism studies (RPTS). But again, such moves tend to be multidisciplinary in orientation *unless* the student is challenged with having to develop a new theoretical or methodological approach due to the inadequacy of existing knowledge. This direction thus represents the ME study route.

- Within RPTS, this challenge has been encountered, encouraging some students to take courses in other departments and to develop new and innovative research approaches. This is the second route, i.e., building IE knowledge. For instance, Kim (2004) offered new reflections bridging serious leisure theory (from "leisure studies") and festival participation in tourism, drawing upon sociology, social psychology, and leisure studies. The potential for interdisciplinarity in such studies, again, is limited to the student's own initiative and that of his peers and thesis/dissertation advisors. Attention to developing a comprehensive IE curriculum approach (versus the ME focus generally present in tourism and recreation programs) is currently lacking. The development of the certificate programs described earlier indicates that there is growing awareness, interest, and effort in building cross-disciplinary linkages between departments and colleges (though these certificate programs are presently multidisciplinary in character).

Cross-campus linkages also add to the potential for developing greater interdisciplinarity in teaching and learning. The College of Architecture and the Department of Recreation, Park, and Tourism Sciences are both members of the Melbern G. Glasscock Center for the Humanities. As the center's website notes: "The Glasscock Center is dedicated to fostering and celebrating the humanities and humanities research among the community of scholars at Texas A&M University and in the world beyond the academy" (retrieved January 21, 2005, from www.tamu.educhr). The center's activities include regular seminars and symposia that attract a cross-disciplinary set of faculty members and students from history, anthropology, tourism studies, architecture and urban planning, philosophy, political science, English and performance studies, etc. Such linkages bode well for developing sustainability-oriented IE programs that dedicate adequate attention to social and cultural concerns (in addition to economic and environmental ones).

There is therefore a wide range of course offerings and cross-campus linkages that could be used to develop comprehensive IE and ME programs oriented towards sustainable tourism development. Within RPTS, for instance, course offerings include tourism impacts and tourism marketing (course instructors trained in management), ecotourism and conservation courses (course instructor trained in anthropology, and conservation as well), environmental impacts of tourism (course instructors trained in geography and in greenways/urban parks planning), national parks management (course instructor trained in zoology and/or experience in national parks policy and management). From a sustainable tourism and management perspective, two areas of IE curriculum development offer significant opportunities for program development:

IE Specialization: Sustainable Destination Management

A good interdisciplinary program would aim for students to graduate with a Master's or Ph.D. degree in tourism planning, and sustainable destination management. The Master's degree would be more hands-on (experience-based) than the Ph.D., which would require a strong theoretical component in addition to field-based experience. Developing a community-based strategy for managing tourism growth, for instance, would be guided by principles of sustainable tourism, practical knowledge of the location and its people (local knowledge, socio-economic, and cultural concerns), as well as planning and impact management skills and tools (e.g., monitoring and indicator development). The interdisciplinary curriculum would include a selection of required and optional courses from key (multi-)disciplinary areas and programs, plus core IE courses related to planning (strategic management and urban planning), historic preservation, environmental management, marketing, and community development.

The IE facilitator would be familiar with both qualitative and quantitative research, i.e., develop appropriate research skills for diverse tasks. An interdisciplinary expert (IE) (student) from this program would therefore be familiar with planning theory and policy, would have some competency in marketing planning, systems modeling, and integrated destination management, and would be able to facilitate the development of a strategic tourism plan. But such an IE would not be able to develop a detailed urban design plan or even a comprehensive community plan, nor a detailed destination or organizational marketing plan (at least, not without training/skills acquired before entering the IE track). Disciplinary expertise, if required, could be provided by retaining a disciplinary expert (DE) or a ME. A cross-disciplinary team managed by the IE could play a useful advisory or active role in destination management.

IE Specialization: Ecotourism and Conservation

Similarly, an ecotourism planner or manager would be trained with a wide-ranging knowledge-base in ecotourism and sustainable development. The curriculum includes critical social theory and specific methodological tools and technical skills (e.g., ecolodge design, certification, standards, and sustainable

Table 10.5 Examples of cross-disciplinary works on modernity, nature, (eco)-tourism, and sustainable development/planning

	Descriptive and applied, managerial (nature as a given)	Theoretical (leisure, recreation, tourism)	Theoretical (sociological, philosophical, political theory, environmental studies, cultural geography)	Critical theoretical (critical theory [CT], critical social and political theory)	Concepts and critical concerns (CT, social theory, cultural studies, post-structuralism, postmodernism)
Modernity and society	WCED (1987)	Dann (1996); Rojek & Urry (1997); Urry (1995); Wang (2000).	Foucault (1980; 1995); Lash and Urry (1994)	Habermas (1978); Horkheimer and Adorno (1979); Ritzer (1996)	Instrumental reason; autonomous rational subject; ideological domination, subjection, surveillance
Environmental management, National Parks, nature, wilderness	Sellars (1997)	Rosenzweig and Blackmar (1992)	Nash (1967); Oelshlager (1991)	Darier (1999); Olwig and Olwig (1979).	Social and political constructions of nature; prediction and control of nature; ecological modernization
Tourism and ecotourism	Fennell (1999); Hall (2000); Weaver (2001)	Britton (1991); Dann (1996a; 1996b); Hollinshead (1999); Franklin (2003)	—	Mowforth and Munt (2003) (applying Bourdieu's theory of distinction); Sharpley (1996)	Production and consumption of tourist experience, representation of nature, ethnicities and cultures.

energy programs). In addition, the student would possess a comprehensive understanding of the meaning of wilderness, the social construction of nature, and the importance of the ecotourism "experience" (Table 10.5). Table 10.5 applies to both ME and IE study streams. In other words, all sustainability-oriented students would be exposed to critical as well as non-critical perspectives on nature, commodification, modernity, and society (e.g., perspectives of human–nature relationships through modernity, the scientific method of studying natural phenomena and objects, changing use and conceptions of wilderness and nature.

Tables 10.4 and 10.5 reflect accumulated insights and issues drawn from various disciplinary areas and fields of study. These can be used as part of course objectives and readings to inform ecotourism development and research from a multidisciplinary perspective, and can be used to create new (interdisciplinary) avenues for understanding the use and formation of natural areas, as well as the practice of ecotourism. For instance, drawing upon postcolonial studies and theories of subjection and power (Foucault, 1990, influencing new theoretical perspectives on power in tourism, e.g., Hollinshead, 1999; Mowforth and Munt, 2003; Urry, 1990), a synthesis of micro-level practices and macro-level historical influences produces a new picture of ecotourism, one that is critical and yet enabling with respect to human-ecological relationships.

Future Directions and Emergent Issues

As tourism has continued to grow in local and global importance, the study of tourism has evolved gradually and steadily in colleges and universities. Special areas of study or concentration in tourism-related areas are housed within, for example, management, anthropology, geography, and sociology. Many of these program areas have begun to provide certification and degree programs oriented towards tourism. Our chapter indicates there are at least two important frameworks worth investigating for cross-disciplinary tourism pedagogy— the first is *multidisciplinary* while the second is *interdisciplinary* (to use the distinction made by scholars previously). Contextualized to a particular educational and cultural setting, either or both may be appropriate to implement as a framework for developing a tourism curriculum.

The complexity, interdependencies, and interrelationships of the tourism system as described at the beginning of this chapter indicates that fostering interdisciplinarity may be necessary for the success of sustainability-oriented programs. "Tourism studies" developed within more functionally oriented recreation, park, and leisure programs (such as the forest-recreation/natural resource influences on RPTS at TAMU) tend to be driven by ME approaches focused on management, marketing, and economic development, even though political science, performance studies, ethics, and philosophy (among others) are highly pertinent to sustainable tourism development. A key area of future investigation lies in identifying trends and barriers towards interdisciplinary and multidisciplinary forms of sustainable tourism education.

The potential for developing IE knowledge that bridges tourism, planning, and historic preservation is encouraging due to (a) the wide range of course offerings, (b) an organizational culture that supports cross-disciplinary research and learning, and (c) increasing awareness of the need for new integrated approaches to planning and managing for sustainability in a post 9–11 world. Certificate programs like the historic preservation and sustainable urbanism programs offer potential for fostering interdisciplinary research and education (even though current awareness and support seem to be more multidisciplinary). Cross-sharing of methodologies, greater understanding of qualitative research, and philosophy of social science courses to offset the traditional preference for quantitative courses is particularly important (Jamal and Everett, 2004). The support of department heads and university administrators is crucial to the task of building a cross-disciplinary knowledge base:

> The statement is frequently made that society has problems while universities have departments. Hence societal issues (and learning) are short circuited by the failure to bring interdisciplinary thinking to the table. Departmental course offerings are made stronger when the course are managed in such a way that these interactions are built into course structures. (Dr. O'Leary, Department Head, RPTS, Personal Communication, 1/24/05)

Much greater attention has thus to be paid to program development for sustainable tourism development and management. The examples provided earlier indicate that multidisciplinary education pathways are being created, but they have yet to adopt the kind of interdisciplinarity called for by Leiper (1981) and others. Moreover, while our two program examples focused on planning and historic preservation, it is important to note that such systems are embedded within ecological systems. The development of holistic sustainability-oriented programs should be framed within politicized ecological-economic and social-cultural paradigms. A number of issues are summarized here for future consideration:

- Multidisciplinary curricula need to clearly identify the key objectives (outcomes), skill development, and theoretical paradigms pursued in the program. The question "what and whose interests are being met through this program?" is a useful one for both the ME and IE program.
- What issues revolve around the location of IE and ME programs? How does it influence program outcomes, course selection, and delivery for IE/ME curricula to be housed within a particular discipline, college, institute, or as a separate entity (Echtner and Jamal, 1997)?
- What are the most effective avenues for developing "sustainable

tourism" paradigms and practitioners? What cross-programs, cross-campus and administrative linkages are most helpful?

- What combination of theory, applied work, and praxis best suit a ME or IE curriculum aimed at training sustainable tourism managers or researchers?
- As "tourism studies" evolves from a pre-paradigmatic to a paradigmatic stage, it will have to grapple with a key issue related to research, education, and practice. Should the field nurture programs that develop interdisciplinary *generalists*, cross-disciplinary *experts*, or both?
- Administrative challenges will also need to be faced by programs attempting to cultivate cross-linkages with other disciplines and related centers. One of the most difficult problems with cross-disciplinary education is working academic schedules so that students can:
  (i) get the course they want and desire, despite the inevitable course cancellation or scheduling challenge, and
  (ii) obtain support and recognition for the innovations they contribute towards developing interdisciplinary theoretical frameworks and methodologies.

Notes

1. For the purpose of our discussion, we will take "scientific" here to mean both social scientific as well as scientific information, and methodologically, quantitative and qualitative methodologies.
2. While the Sustainable Urbanism program is listed as "interdisciplinary," this may mean "multidisciplinary" in the context of this chapter, following Leiper (1981).
3. The readings in 10.4 can be applied from either an IE or ME approach. Also see Jamal and Lee (2003).

References

Bourdieu, P. (1977). *Outline of a theory of practice*. Cambridge: Cambridge University Press.

Bourdieu, P. (1984). *Distinction: A critique of the judgement of taste*. London: Routledge and Kegan Paul.

Bramwell, B., Henry, I., Jackson, G., Prat, A., Richards, G., and van der Straaten, J. (Eds.) (1996). *Sustainable tourism management: Principles and practice*. Tilburg: Tilburg University Press.

Britton, S. (1991). Tourism, capital and place: Towards a critical geography of tourism. *Environment and Planning D: Society and Space, 9*, 451–478.

Dann, G. (1996). *The language of tourism—A sociolinguistic analysis*. Wallingford, UK: CAB International.

Dann, G. (1999). Theoretical issues for tourism's future development: Identifying the agenda. In D. G. Pearce, and R. W. Butler (Eds.), *Contemporary issues in tourism development* (pp. 13–30). London: Routledge.

Darier, E. (Ed.) (1999a). *Discourses of the environment*. Oxford: Blackwell Publishers.

Echtner, C., and Jamal, T. (1997). The disciplinary dilemma of tourism studies. *Annals of Tourism Research, 24*, 868–883.

Fennell, D. (1999). *Ecotourism: An introduction*. London and New York: Routledge.

Flyvberg, B. (2001). *Making social science matter*. Cambridge: Cambridge University Press.

Foucault, M. (1980). *Power/knowledge: Selected interviews and other writings*. New York: Pantheon.

Foucault, M. (1995). *Discipline and punish: The birth of the prison* (2nd edn). New York: Vintage Books.

Franklin, A. (2003). *Tourism: An introduction.* London and Thousand Oaks, CA: Sage.

Habermas, J. (1978). *Knowledge and human interests* (2nd ed.). Translated by J. J. Shapiro. Boston: Beacon Press.

Habermas, J. (1995). *The theory of communicative action.* Cambridge: Polity Press.

Hall, S. (Ed.) (1997). *Representation: Cultural representation and signifying practices.* London and Thousand Oaks, CA: Sage.

Hall, C. M. (2000). *Tourism planning: Policies, processes and relationships.* London and New York: Prentice Hall.

Hall, C. M., and Page, S. J. (1999). *The geography of tourism and recreation: Environment, space and place.* London and New York: Routledge.

Holden, A. (2003). In need of new environmental ethics for tourism? *Annals of Tourism Research, 30*(1), 94–108.

Hollinshead, K. (1999). Surveillance of the worlds of tourism: Foucault and the eye-of-power. *Tourism Management, 20,* 7–23.

Horkheimer, M., and Adorno, T. W. (1979). *Dialectic of enlightenment.* New York: Continuum.

Jafari, J. (1991). Tourism social science. *Annals of Tourism Research, 18,* 1–9.

Jafari, J. (2001). The scientification of tourism. In V. L. Smith, and M. Brent (Eds.), *Hosts and guests revisited: Tourism issues of the 21st century* (pp. 28–41). New York: Cognizant Communication Corporation.

Jafari, J., and Ritchie, J. R. B. (1981). Toward a framework for tourism education: Problems and prospects. *Annals of Tourism Research, 8*(1), 13–34.

Jamal, T. (2005). Virtue ethics and sustainable tourism pedagogy: Phronesis, principles and practice. *Journal of Sustainable Tourism, 12*(6), 530–545.

Jamal, T., and Everett, J. (2004). Resisting rationalization in the natural and academic lifeworld: Critical tourism research or hermeneutic charity? *Current Issues in Tourism, 7*(1), 1–19.

Jamal, T., and Lee, J. L. (2003). Towards a better theoretical base for tourist motivations: Integrating macro and micro approaches. *Tourism Analysis, 8*(1), 47–59.

Jamal, T., Everett, J., and Dann, G. M. (2003). Ecological rationalization and performative resistance in natural area destinations. *Tourist Studies, 3*(2), 143–169.

Jourdan, D. (2004). Planning to reduce worry: Designing an intergenerational planning process to lessen relocation-related anxieties experienced by those displaced in the pursuit of a HOPE VI Revitalization Grant. Ph.D. dissertation, Florida State University.

Kim, H. (2004). Serious leisure, participation, and experience in tourism: Authenticity and ritual in a Renaissance festival. Department of Recreation, Park, and Tourism Sciences, Texas A&M University, College Station, Texas.

Kuhn, T. (1970). *The structure of scientific revolutions.* Chicago: University of Chicago Press.

Lash, S., and Urry, J. (1994). *Economies of science and space* (2nd ed.). London: Sage.

Leiper, N. (1981). Towards a cohesive curriculum in tourism: The case for a distinctive discipline. *Annals of Tourism Research, 7,* 69–84.

Leiper, N. (1990). Tourism systems: An interdisciplinary study (Occasion Papers No. 2). Palmerston, New Zealand: Department of Management Systems, Massey University.

Leiper, N. (2000). An emerging discipline. Rejoinder and commentary. *Annals of Tourism Research, 27*(3), 805–809.

Mowforth, M., and Munt, I. (2003). *Tourism and sustainability in the Third World: Development and new tourism in the Third World* (2nd ed.). London: Routledge.

Nash, R. (1967). *Wilderness and the American Mind* (3rd ed.). New Haven: Yale University Press.

Oelschlaeger, M. (1991). *The idea of wilderness: From pre-history to the age of ecology.* New Haven and London: Yale University Press.

Olwig, K. L., and Olwig, K. F. (1979). Underdevelopment and the development of "natural" park ideology. *Antipode, 11,* 16–25.

Prezclawski, K. (1993). Tourism as the subject of interdisciplinary research. In D. Pearce and R. Butler (Eds.). *Tourism research: Critiques and challenges* (pp. 9–19). London: Routledge.

Ritzer, G. (1996). *The McDonaldization of society: An investigation into the changing character of contemporary life* (rev. ed.). Thousand Oaks, CA: Pine Forge Press.

Rojek, C., and Urry, J. (Eds.) (1997). *Touring cultures: Transformations of travel and theory.* London: Routledge.

Rosenzweig, R., and Blackmar, E. (1992). *Park and the people.* Ithaca, NY: Cornell University Press.

Sellars, R. W. (1997). *Preserving nature in the National Parks: A history.* New Haven and London: Yale University Press.

Sharpley, R. (1996). Tourism and consumer culture in postmodern society. In M. Robinson, N. Evans, and P. Callaghan (Eds.), *Tourism and cultural change*. Newcastle: University of Northumbria.

Tribe, J. (1997). The indiscipline of tourism. *Annals of Tourism Research, 24*, 637–657.

Tribe, J. (2002a). Education for ethical tourism action. *Journal of Sustainable Tourism, 10*(4), 309–324.

UNEP-ICLEI (2003). *Tourism and Local Agenda 21: The role of local authorities in sustainable tourism*. United Nations Environment Program (UNEP) and International Council for Local Environmental Initiatives (ICLEI). Paris: United Nations Publication (UNEP).

Urry, J. (1990). *The tourist gaze: Leisure and travel in contemporary society*. London: Sage.

Urry, J. (1995). *Consuming places*. London: Routledge.

Wang, N. (2000). *Tourism and modernity: A sociological analysis*. Amsterdam: Pergamon.

Weaver, D. (2001). *Ecotourism*. Milton, Qld: John Wiley.

World Commission on Environment and Development (1987). *Our common future*. New York: Oxford University Press.

11

Five Strategic Imperatives for Interdisciplinary Study in Mass Communications/Media Studies in the U.S. and U.K.

Iona College

This chapter addresses a fundamental question: How can the field of mass communications/media studies, which has grown into its own discipline, still benefit from interdisciplinary links with other university departments and research approaches from other fields? Students who graduate from a mass communications program in the U.S. or U.K. today face significantly different challenges than did the cohort of students in the 1980s and even the 1990s. Unprecedented changes in global economy and technology, as well as new cultural, ethnic, and ethical issues worldwide, have altered the landscape for studying mass communications in the U.S. and U.K. This new direction calls for greater focus on an interdisciplinary study of the liberal arts in the mass communications/media studies curriculum. In addition, more interdisciplinary research and teaching are needed to help students grow and succeed in their chosen work.

Researchers may argue that colleges are already accomplishing what is necessary to train their students for the new century. Indeed, colleges and universities in both the U.S and U.K. have made strides in this regard and improved their core curriculum. Nevertheless, the essential questions that fuel the work of educators and researchers include: Are students being adequately prepared for their first job or for life? Can they grapple with world issues and concerns that impact upon the future of democracy and freedom by merely taking one or two courses in history or political science? Are students evolving into competent problem-solvers, critical thinkers, and creative individuals or just adding courses to their transcripts that seem to fill these roles? Faculty members need to prepare students not only to compete for jobs in a new global economy, but also to have the intellectual breadth of knowledge to understand complex issues, become creative knowledge-seekers, and behave ethically. Students require preparation to become world citizens who will positively contribute to the organizations they join and, in turn, benefit society.

This chapter suggests five strategic imperatives for the study of mass communications/media studies in the U.S. and U.K. that will support the important role of interdisciplinary study to extend the theoretical foundations and research methods of the field as well as global knowledge in the twenty-first century. The five imperatives are:

- Embracing an interdisciplinary approach to the study and research of mass communications/media studies by forging an alliance with the fields of anthropology, sociology, political science, information technology, and education;
- Providing internships in more than one field of study;
- Improving ways of knowing and learning in the classroom;
- Stressing global literacy as an essential part of the college experience; and
- Addressing issues of discipline and assessment in the curriculum and ascertaining its ultimate achievement.

Learning Across the Disciplines

The first imperative involves embracing an interdisciplinary approach in the curriculum. Interdisciplinary study typically bridges multiple disciplines and involves data collection and analysis from more than one research tradition. The field of mass communications/media studies has early roots in political science, sociology, psychology, and rhetoric and speech. It offers an inter-disciplinary focus and is itself the object of interdisciplinary study (McQuail 1985). However, the discipline appears to be drifting away from these liberal arts roots while forging its own niche as a self-contained discipline. To meet students' growing demands for more relevant courses that can lead directly to jobs, the discipline has often sacrificed creating links to other university departments that could broaden its students' knowledge and mold them into true world citizens. Corporations, non-profit organizations, advertising and public relations agencies, broadcast networks, newspapers, and magazines are in great need of talented, creative, and widely educated students who can adapt to any environment and welcome change in a work world that reflects an inter-disciplinary approach. Unlike their academic counterparts, few organizations today operate in a "silo" mentality; to achieve success, their workers must perform tasks in multiple departments with workers possessing diverse skills and knowledge.

While many courses in a mass communications/media curriculum may help students win their first jobs, a broader interdisciplinary education in conjunction with practicum courses will move them into more meaningful higher-level jobs. Their broader knowledge will arm them to become true knowledge-seekers and problem-solving thinkers who are more aware of cultural relationships and boundaries that shape today's world.

Political Science Perspective

One certain way to encourage this potential is to forge stronger links with political science departments so that students will not only learn the nature and effects of propaganda and persuasion, but also the process by which political systems in the U.S. and around the world determine policy that influences how governments function at their best and worst. Future policymakers with training in both the mass communications discipline and the political process will draw from a much wider context to suggest solutions for international problems. Students inclined to enter the public service sector with a mass communications degree would benefit from this cross-training as well.

Sociological Imagination

Undergraduates who expect to spend much of their lives helping organizations build relationships with global customers, partners, and citizens would benefit from acquiring a strong theoretical grounding in how the social world works —its norms, rituals, and traditions—and an understanding of the impact of social issues on communications. For example, future journalists might become more analytical observers of the world they cover by understanding the sociology of media organizations along with the mechanics of writing a news story. They might also be better served by spending more class time reading the works of Weber and Durkheim and less time on calculating the readability formulas of Flesh and Gunning. This does not underestimate the importance of the mechanics of journalism education, especially as employers insist on these skills for the marketplace. Nevertheless, mechanics alone is inadequate; students need to learn to analyze social and organizational issues in order to write more creatively and insightfully about them. Because sociologists have studied the impact of television, media, and news reporting as well as the influence of culture on society (Gans, 1979), their crucial findings and perceptions should be integrated into the communications courses of traditional college curricula.

Learning about Human Nature and Society

One of the principal figures in the early history of mass communication was anthropologist Gregory Bateson, who featured relational communication based on cybernetic theory in the study of mass communications (Rogers, 1994). Thus, the study of anthropology would demonstrate to students how tribal societies form opinions and co-exist or why certain cultures view others with favor or disdain. This field offers practical advice and knowledge on how students can create communication campaigns in the profit and non-profit sectors with a stronger global understanding of human nature.

The Technology Perspective

The more technology undergoes social change, the more critical it is for the discipline to retain links with university departments that are up-to-date with such changes. Information technology faculty, for example, can be an important resource for mass communication students in helping them master new technologies and articulating the implications of their use in the marketplace. They could suggest curricular changes to new media faculty and collaborate on team-taught survey courses in technology applications. Through this joint effort, mass communications students would be exposed to the most recent advances in technology applications as they prepare to enter the workforce or attend graduate school.

Media Literacy Perspective

Finally, a joint effort with the education department on teaching media literacy would contribute significantly to university life as well as society. While mass communications students could benefit from new instructional technology approaches offered by the education department, young teachers could benefit from the expertise of mass communications scholars in media literacy. As a result, new teachers, especially at the high school level, would be better equipped to understand the workings of media on a much broader scale than they were previously taught.

While students typically can declare a minor in a separate field of study or take courses in a related field at many colleges and universities in the U.S. and U.K., the courses are not necessarily interdisciplinary nor do students make such cross-discipline connections. One solution to encourage an exchange of ideas beyond the core curriculum is to break down department silos and allow mass communications students to explore new and linked learning environments. Thus, they would become better equipped as world citizens, not merely as consumers of knowledge.

Experiential Learning Across the Disciplines

The second strategic imperative is to create an administrative protocol that allows mass communications/new media students to experience the power of internships in more than one field of study. Most mass communications departments now in the U.S. and U.K. urge their students to complete internships in a subspecialty such as public relations, advertising, journalism broadcasting, and new media. With such work experience to complement college courses, students can make more intelligent decisions about their career plans. Another advantage of an internship in a subspecialty is its socialization of students in a professional area of interest. However, by adding a second internship to the curriculum for credit or pass/fail in a field outside but closely aligned to the major, students would meet professionals in that field and extend their own expertise to another field that complements their learning in mass communications. As illustration, a public relations student major who would like a career in government service would be assigned as an administrative intern to a government agency for the management team, learning about the operations of that agency. The student's second internship would be with a public relations firm that works closely with the agency or government clients. With this dual learning and training, the student would be better positioned to create well-designed communications plans which meet the needs of the agency or clients. As another example of dual training in internships, an advertising or new media student major who wants to have a non-profit career would be first assigned to a non-profit agency with the management team to learn how a non-profit functions on different projects. In the second internship assignment, the student would move to an advertising agency to create promotional pieces that enhance the agency's image and raise money for the agency's primary cause. This cross-training in two aligned disciplines would provide the student with a greater breadth of knowledge previously unavailable in the current curriculum.

This cross-disciplinary approach through internships is not easy to accomplish in an academic setting. On the one hand, its greatest administrative challenge is to require different academic departments to cooperate and share resources and faculty to help students learn about an allied field. On the other, more positive side, however, colleges or universities can promote this dual-learning approach among parents, prospective students, and employers. Nevertheless, students would be the main beneficiaries of this interdisciplinary approach to experiential learning, as they would receive a foundation that launches their early careers and sustains them throughout their lives.

Other Ways of Knowing and Learning in the Classroom

The third strategic perspective is to improve ways of knowing and learning in the classroom. It has become necessary to challenge a college's traditional organization around disciplines and to question whether this structure is best for giving students the broadest view of an academic discipline. On some level, students are aware that the real world is not neatly divided into categories called history, physics, psychology, politics, and literature. Each field is alive with human practitioners, all of whom offer different worldviews and experiences which draw from across disciplines. In addition, prospective employers expect newly hired college graduates to understand new concepts by gaining knowledge from departments as diverse as information science, marketing, accounting, and public relations in order to function in their chosen field of interest.

In a study conducted by the Harvard Graduate School of Education which examined the conditions under which students learn best both inside and outside the classroom, "many seniors single out interdisciplinary courses as the course that means the most to them" (Light, 2001, p. 126). While students are satisfied with in-depth education in one or two disciplines including a minor field, Light points out that they also want more exposure to different aspects of the curriculum.

Faculty members and administrators can give students a cross-cutting experience by promoting team teaching across the disciplines. In this approach, students are more apt to synthesize ideas while drawing on their faculty's experiences of introducing divergent viewpoints into the classroom. A good example of this would be a communications professor and a political science professor who team-teach a campaigns course, with subjects ranging from public opinion dynamics, persuasion theories, and communication strategies to voting behavior, planning, and measurement standards. This collaborative learning would clarify in dimensional form how campaigns are researched, planned, organized, and conducted.

Team learning is becoming an integral part of the workplace landscape in the twenty-first century. As companies, government agencies, and non-profit organizations establish high-performance teams to tackle major projects, students exposed to interdisciplinary learning in and out of the classroom may have a competitive edge in those settings. At least, they will become more conscious of how the media and other disciplines are interconnected.

In addition to team work, another technique to improve ways of knowing and learning in the classroom is to create learning communities within the discipline. A learning community typically links two or more disciplines around a common theme and arranges for students to attend courses and live together on campus. While one early goal of learning communities was to improve student retention rates on college campuses, they have also helped students in mass communications programs to understand more fully the relationships between their discipline and work in other fields on campus. In experiments with learning communities, American colleges have found that their students benefit from shared learning and greater insight into the media environment. Blanchard and Christ (1993) suggest that not only is building bridges vital between communications departments and the academy, but connections should also be constructed within the communications discipline itself. Thus, mass communications/media studies programs in the U.S. and U.K. can increase their effectiveness by identifying the benefits of team teaching, team learning, and learning communities, and incorporating them into the curriculum.

Global Literacy and the Global Village

The fourth strategic imperative is to make global literacy essential to the college experience. For students in a mass communications/media studies program, global literacy involves understanding national interdependence, interacting and communicating with diverse peoples, and creating and distributing content persuasively to audiences of all sizes. Globally literate students should think with an international mindset that values the cultures and customs of other nations. In addition, they should participate in teams where diversity of talent and nationality is the rule rather than the exception.

Students are now living in the "global village," the phrase so aptly coined by Marshall McLuhan in the 1960s. Information flows freely and rapidly across borders, creating instant access to international news events. For global literacy to become integral to the college experience, faculty members must discover ways to make it relevant in the classroom. One step is to invite scholars from the international relations department to share their global perspectives and suggest pertinent activities. Another step is to establish global exchange programs and cultural and international events which can allow students to travel abroad and begin applying learned skills in an international context. A third step is to train students to speak, write, and read a second language to facilitate their travel and enrich their experiences through greater comprehension and communication. Mass communications/media studies programs need champions of global literacy on the campus who recognize that when students gain a global perspective of current issues, they will more likely thrive internationally. Many courses in the mass communications discipline can be modified to include a segment on global literacy, which explores a range of world and cultural issues as students progress through their major. Service-learning projects are another tool with which colleges can promote global literacy. For example, colleges in or near large urban centers can set up programs that incorporate immersion into encounters with more varied nationalities and cultures than are available on campus.

In exchange programs with other colleges, visiting scholars can be recruited to spend one or two semesters on campus mentoring students in the mass communications/media studies department. Similarly, mass communications faculty can spend a semester overseas interacting and conducting research with foreign students. Mass communications/media studies departments can also establish web-based initiatives to join students from many countries with local nationals. Finally, faculty can apply for grants from international organizations that encourage cross-cultural skills training and open new areas of communication research in developing countries or "hot spots" such as the Middle East. With a global literacy perspective in the curriculum, students can be trained not only to interpret behaviors in different cultural contexts, but also to build meaningful relationships with others in foreign lands.

Rigor and Assessment in the Curriculum

The fifth strategic imperative concerns the all-important issue of rigor and assessment in the mass communications/media studies curriculum. Colleges and universities in the U.S. and U.K. are gradually ensuring that undergraduate programs offer significant experiences and learning outcomes for their students. The faculty-at-large are also being challenged to provide students with deep learning experiences that compel them to challenge assumptions, create new ways of thinking, and take risks in the classroom. To create an environment of excellence, the best college teachers are becoming increasingly familiar with best learning practices and the conditions in which such learning will flourish in the classroom (Bain, 2004).

Mass communications/media studies programs remain popular on U.S. campuses, and are growing in popularity in the U.K. For the most part, the field of mass communications in the U.S. has achieved parity with the more established fields in the liberal arts such as psychology, sociology, and history. Its scholars are widely published and its students are some of the brightest on campus. In the U.K., however, some critics have labeled media studies and mass communications programs "Mickey Mouse" courses—that is, they lack rigor and are not seriously considered by the academic community. Yet, this judgment has been vigorously challenged by U.K. media studies scholars who demonstrate the field's significant relevance to students and faculty in other disciplines. The field's mainstream history for more than 40 years has recognized strong traditions of excellence on many U.K. campuses (Baty, 2003). Equally important for the field's credibility is that some of the more interesting approaches to the study of mass communications/media studies have been offered by U.K. scholars at worldwide academic forums and conferences.

An organization at the forefront of improving the quality and stature of mass communications programs in the U.S. is the Accrediting Council on Education and Journalism and Mass Communication (ACEJMC). It judges programs against objectives that institutions set for themselves and against standards that the Council regulates to prepare students for professional careers in journalism and mass communications. The Council adopted new standards that went into effect in September 2004 for accreditation reviews in 2005–2006. Colleges and universities that apply for accreditation must submit documentation to meet the standards in the following nine areas:

- Mission, governance, and administration;
- Curriculum and instruction;
- Diversity and inclusiveness;
- Full-time and part-time faculty;
- Scholarship, research, creative and professional activity;
- Student services;
- Resources, facilities, and equipment;
- Professional and public service; and
- Assessment of learning outcomes.

The Council currently accredits 105 schools and departments of journalism and mass communications in the U.S. and one program overseas (more than 400 colleges and universities offer one or more mass communications programs). ACEJMC evaluates Bachelor's degree and professional Master's degree programs.

Another valuable tool for evaluating mass communications/media studies programs is the internship program in such areas as advertising, public relations, journalism, radio, television, film, production, and web communications. These students often complete extensive reports on their experiences that allow the college to measure the effectiveness of its program in the workplace. Feedback from employers who hire interns can also assist the faculty and department to upgrade the curriculum and make necessary changes. Some colleges have used advisory councils composed of industry experts to shape the mass communications curriculum and create a "sounding board" for new ideas and research.

Other tools with which college faculty and administrators can measure the success of their programs are professional portfolios, alumni/employer surveys, and capstone courses (Blanchard and Christ, 1993). Many colleges now require their students to develop a student portfolio documenting their class or internship assignments that demonstrate professional competence in their major field of study. Students can also show their portfolios to prospective employers during job interviews. Similarly, portfolios demonstrate levels of student learning that senior faculty in the department can assess. The alumni/employer survey is an excellent way to collect feedback on the mass communications program. Young alumni out of college less than three years and senior alumni in the workforce 10 to 20 years can be rich sources of information on how well the college or university is training candidates for the workplace and life itself. A poor report card by junior and senior alumni members may indicate the need for a major program revision. Employers in the profit, non-profit, and government sectors should also be surveyed regularly to gauge the quality of students completing their programs at U.S. and U.K. institutions. Finally, capstone courses can help faculty ascertain the value of the mass communications curriculum. Typically, students undertake major research projects for their capstones in which they integrate theoretical knowledge from coursework with applied research skills on a topic in their area of specialization.

Summary

The five strategic imperatives outlined in this chapter are designed to stimulate discussion and debate on the value of interdisciplinary study in the field of mass communications/media studies. Each imperative challenges college faculty and administrators to move beyond comfort zones and "silos," and apply these approaches to the classroom and field work. Both profit and non-profit organizations in the twenty-first century will demand that students adapt to changing global conditions, participate in interdisciplinary teams, solve problems and create new ideas with critical thinking, and be increasingly culturally sensitive. Mass communications/media studies programs in the U.S. and

U.K. can serve as models to lead students into successful learning through interdisciplinary study.

References

Baetens, J., and Lambert J. (Eds.) (2000). *The future of cultural studies: Essays in honour of Joris Vlasselafrs*. Leuven, Belgium: Leuven University Press.

Bain, K. (2004). *What the best college teachers do*. Cambridge, MA: Harvard University Press.

Baty, P. (2003, December 19–26). "The 'joke' field with serious prospects." *The Times Higher Education Supplement*. p. 11.

Blanchard, R., and Christ, W. (1993). *Media education and the liberal arts*. Hillsdale, NJ: Lawrence Erlbaum Associates.

Dennis, E. E. (1989). *Technological convergence and communication education*. New York: Gannett Center for Media Education.

Gans, H. (1979). *Deciding what's news*. New York: Pantheon.

Kamalipour, Y. (2002). *Global communications*. Belmont, CA: Wadsworth/Thomas Learning.

Light, R. (2001). *Making the most of college: Students speak their minds*. Cambridge, MA: Harvard University Press.

McQuail, D. (1985). Sociology of mass communication. *Annual Review of Sociology, 11*, 93–111.

McPhail, T. (2002). *Global communications: Theories, stakeholders, and trends*. Boston, MA: Allyn & Bacon.

Miller, T. (Ed.) (2001). *A companion to cultural studies*. Oxford, UK: Blackwell Publishers.

Murray, M., and Ferri, A. (1992). *Teaching mass communication: A guide to better instruction*. Westport, CT: Praeger.

Rogers, E. M. (1994). *A history of communication study*. New York: Free Press.

Tysome, T. (2004, January 23). "Do they deserve to be degrees?" *The Times Higher Education Supplement*. p. 8.

12
Interdisciplinary Science
A Case Study in the Management of Innovation

DEREK RAINE

i-Science Centre, University of Leicester

This case study will look at the context in which the introduction of an integrated, interdisciplinary science curriculum has been brought about in one U.K. institution and at the management of that change.

The context of this work is the relative decline in recruitment in the U.K. to science programs in higher education (HE). As a fraction of the total undergraduate entry, the contribution from physical sciences and mathematics declined by a factor of about three in the period 1985–2000 and the decline in biological sciences was almost as steep.[1] One factor that has been cited in various attempts to reverse the situation is the perceived lack of relevance of science amongst school students and a lack of excitement in the way the subject is taught.[2] There is a widespread belief that the "hard sciences" are difficult, to the extent that many people seem to think that "hard" refers to the degree of difficulty! Against this background, there is little to support the view that the relative decline in the numbers wishing to study a single science discipline to degree level can be reversed by haranguing students about how interesting these subjects really are. A lot of subjects are interesting, but that does not mean one wants to study them exclusively for the rest of one's academic life.

To some extent, this issue can be addressed through joint degrees and there is some evidence for this in the growth of U.K. programs in natural science. The problem with most natural science programs, however, is that they are amalgamations of parts of existing single subject degrees with little or no integration. In that sense they represent merely a "delayed choice" option and may largely cannibalize existing programs. A certain amount of market-analysis[3] seems to show a role for a more genuinely interdisciplinary approach. This would address the issue of attracting a new cohort of students to science by focusing on real-world problems, which are usually interdisciplinary in nature. It is of interest to note just how many of the outreach activities designed to attract pupils to science are interdisciplinary (particle physics notwithstanding).

In order to move towards an integrated program, the academic challenge is:

- To design a curriculum for a three- or four-year undergraduate program in interdisciplinary science;
- To ensure that the program is fully integrated;
- To allow flexibility within the program in order to provide an element of student choice;
- To ensure that employability issues are fully addressed;
- To address the issue of student diversity within the program;
- To achieve this within available resources.

In addition, we have the management challenge:

- To convince the university to invest in the development;
- To find a viable management structure within the existing organization.

Finally, there is the obvious marketing challenge to convince employers, teachers, parents, and potential students.

This chapter will deal first with the management and marketing aspects and then move on to the curriculum challenge.

In the case to be reported here at the University of Leicester, the "buy-in" of the key players within the university resulted directly from the continuing relative under-recruitment in home students in science across the faculty. It was widely felt that an integrated science program might be able to recruit sufficient numbers of appropriately qualified students. This would avoid the alternative strategy of maintaining recruitment through a general lowering of entry standards, an approach that is not cost-free. Indeed, it is thought that the resources involved in extending the range of student entry qualifications are not necessarily less than those required to develop and deliver a new program. It was widely recognized that such a new program could not be based on existing single subject courses (re-inventing the recently abandoned "combined sciences" programs) if a new cohort of students were to be attracted to science.

The recognition of a common problem is not however the same as agreement on a common solution. Indeed, the search for the magic *Physics with Something Wonderful* program goes on. (Astronomy appears to have filled this role for physics for some time, just as forensic chemistry does for chemistry now.) But it was interesting to discover how many staff were prepared to champion the idea of an interdisciplinary science program.

The first exploratory meetings took place amongst staff in the Department of Physics to establish some basic principles upon which the project might proceed. Two essential pointers were set down. The program would be based on problem-based learning, for reasons I shall discuss below. To provide an integrated interdisciplinary approach all the modules would be new, not reformatted parts of existing modules (even the existing problem-based learning ones). It was also felt that the degree could not be market-tested without a name. A number of suggestions were explored in several meetings, including the usual suspects such as *Science in the Modern World* and so on. Eventually, a long argument about the relative merits of *Integrated Science* and *Interdisciplinary Science* resulted in acceptance of *i*-Science which (perhaps not entirely happily from a brand identity viewpoint) has stuck.

For a time the discussions went round in circles for several reasons. Without a departmental base and students, *i*-Science could not receive resources. (This is, of course, not a logical necessity but rather an aspect of the local culture.) We could have proposed a levy on departments in the faculty, but the notion that the first effect of *i*-Science would be to reduce the resources of already hard-pressed departments would not only not have been an encouraging start in principle, but would have led to practical difficulties of comparability between departments. Eventually, we agreed to an *i*-Science Centre as an entity within the Physics Department funded by accumulated miscellaneous income to the department (essentially from various teaching projects) with a contribution from the university to publicity and marketing and a contribution from faculty funding for its teaching and learning strategy. This has at least allowed the centre to have a legal status within the university, and hence a website, postal address, and such like, and permitted the appointment of a centre manager and secretary, without which the project would be impossible. The development of materials for the program has been funded through departments as far as staff time is concerned, and from support to project LeAP from the national Fund for the Development of Teaching and Learning (FDTL4) as far as some support for the problem-based learning aspects are concerned.

It should be said that this administrative compromise has resulted in the project having the nature of a pilot, with a "beg and borrow" approach to resources.

The marketing aspects have been difficult to say the least, and probably underestimated initially. Reactions to the degree from academics, other professionals, most (but not all) teachers, and employers have been enthusiastically positive. Reaching potential students has been more difficult and it may be necessary to influence them at an earlier stage than at the filling-in of university application forms.

To turn now to the aspects of curriculum development and the academic challenge, the first point to note is that the idea of a more general science program has been raised several times in the past within the university in various contexts. The problem has always been that of designing a program that would provide a range of options for a relatively small cohort of students with a wide range of entry skills, but without additional staff resources. The solution is to start, not within the traditional framework of lecture-based courses, but with a list of varieties of approaches to university teaching. For this it was helpful that the Physics Department core teaching is not in any case lecture-based and the Science Faculty has generally been quite innovative in developing new teaching methods. There was also an existing interest in problem-based learning (PBL) within the Physics Department.

Of the various approaches, resource-based, project-based, case-based, context-based, PBL provides the key to the program. Not only does it solve the problem of viability, but also because it provides a coherent learning environment which aligns the learning outcomes, prior knowledge, content, and assessment regimes. While PBL is often judged to be more resource-intensive than a traditional lecture-based approach for large numbers of students all studying a fixed content, in contrast PBL allows the facilitation of a range of student approaches (equivalent to "options" in the traditional setting) with only marginally increased cost, independent of that range. PBL also provides a coherent learning environment for the embedding of employability skills, crucial to the *i*-Science concept, not least because real-world problems in science are largely interdisciplinary.

A curriculum is, however, more than an arbitrary set of interdisciplinary modules from a random assortment of academic staff, and PBL comes in as many varieties as there are implementations. Involving a range of academic departments that span archaeology to physics and include chemistry, geography, geology, mathematics, and biological sciences in a context that specifies no particular scientific study on entry runs the risk of mounting seven parallel A-level courses. We were assisted by the fact that we could build on the interdisciplinary research base of most of the staff in the *i*-Science Centre. We have identified a very limited core of material that all students will learn and a larger range of content that will be available to chose from. We have then chosen modules to represent various themes, ranging from fundamental theoretical aspects of science at one extreme to technological applications at the other. A matrix of module topics will allow us to see that the core material is covered in a systematic order.

The construction of each module is the responsibility of a three-member teaching team drawn from the three academic departments deemed (sometimes somewhat arbitrarily) to be most relevant. Following the example of Dublin City University[4] we have employed recent graduates in science disciplines to assist with the assembling of material for the modules. Some of this material was tested on volunteer groups before the real students arrived in October 2004.

We adopt the floating facilitator model in which the facilitators will in general not be subject experts, and supplement this with "expert" tutorials. The training of facilitators is in our experience key to the success of PBL. We have prepared training videos under the University of Leicester FDTL-funded[5] LeAP project on PBL,[6] and will draw on our current experience in physics and biological sciences.

Advanced mathematical skills are included as learning outcomes, but not as pre-requisites. This represents an important experiment in several regards. Will the inclusion of mathematics dissuade potential applicants? Can such skills be acquired post A-level by students who have experienced only a limited amount of mathematics on entry? We tackle this by allowing these skills to be acquired over the full three years, rather than, as often happens, towards the start of a degree program. We adopt a user-friendly approach and supply the mathematics teaching on an "as needed" basis. The mathematics is not, however to be taught "in context." We have found that presenting new subject matter in addition to the requisite mathematics compounds the difficulty of both and makes generalization of the mathematics to other contexts problematic for many students. We do, however, endeavor to set the mathematics subject matter within an interesting mathematics context. Aspects of linear algebra can be taught to quite young and not particularly gifted children in the context of iterative maps for fractals, because the students engage with the fascination of the subject matter.

Assessment has proved the greatest bone of contention amongst Centre staff and this is illuminating in the context of PBL. It is sometimes difficult to explain that however impressive the ability to regurgitate facts and information continuously for three hours, there are other ways to impress. On the other hand the standard examination is an efficient way of demonstrating a particular type of individual knowledge. There is therefore a tension between the desire to show that PBL works in conventional terms and the desire to match assessment to the learning outcomes set for the course. It remains to be seen whether the compromise between continuous assessment, including both process and subject knowledge on the one hand and examinations on the other is stable.

Our conclusion is that, given drivers for change that prevision crisis at a stage where resources exist to respond, staff at a research-based university can respond in imaginative and enthusiastic ways to opportunities in learning and teaching that are perceived to have benefits for the community, even where there is an absence of direct rewards to the individuals. We ascribe this to the perception that individual benefits can accrue from improvements to the learning environment. In particular, staff see *i*-Science as an opportunity to offer students a genuine choice of program as opposed to the largely marginal choice of a alternative place to study their speciality. Such change will only come about, however, if it supported through the institution by the provision of resources (for example for recruitment and program management) that allow academic staff to engage intellectually without an overbearing administrative and organizational burden.

Notes

1. *Building a flourishing future: Inquiry into undergraduate physics.* London: Institute of Physics.

2. As the author understands it, this is one of the main motivating factors in the development of the Institute of Physics (IoP) Advanced Physics syllabus and the Salters' Chemistry and Physics syllabi. It also appears as an underlying theme in the Williams enquiry for IoP. The York GCSE program, 21st Century Science, is a clear attempt to address this issue.
3. Unpublished market research carried out on behalf of the IoP New Degrees Working Group (2002).
4. Paul van Kampen at the Physics Department at Dublin City University.
5. Fund for the Development of Teaching and Learning.
6. See http://www.le.ac.uk/leap. [Editorial note: The project ran from 2002 to 2006.]

13
Theory and Practice of Interdisciplinarity in Futures Studies

A. SUNDARAM

Madurai Kamaraj University

Introduction

In the Indian higher education scenario, isolated disciplines continue to hold sway, pretending a "mutually exclusive" posture. The complexity of the society we live in and the range of problems we need to solve warrant new outlooks in teaching and learning. The changed realities and associated complexity levels to be managed now render it imperative that an interdisciplinary approach be embraced in the broadest and deepest possible manner. The multiple disciplines in vogue are reflective of the attempts to fractionally but precisely capture the multifaceted nature of reality and are outcomes of a positivist approach. It would have been infinitely nicer if it were something like a synecdoche where parts can reflect whole and vice versa. But much to our dismay, reality is never equal to the sum of its parts. It is a complex whole that contains multiple elements with varying degrees of interactions and dynamics different as a totality. However exhaustively studied, the dynamics of a single element will always be at variance when it acts within a whole. This system behavior renders isolated disciplines intrinsically inaccurate. The elephant perceived by five blind men was fortunate: it got only five interpretations. (Five academics would have contrived to bring out a minimum of seven!)

The discriminative doctrine, reductionism gave rise to the hydra we have and nurture today, although interestingly it evolved from the original organicism or holism. The key benefits derived from this much maligned, at times much vaunted, approach at today's high school pass out have a few things to teach Aristotle, the encyclopedic ancient. He knows that the earth is round and not flat, the earth orbits around the sun and not otherwise, and the brain is not for cooling the blood. Fragmentation helped in the acquisition of vast data pools on a variety of things and phenomena, extremely sophisticated analytical techniques, profound research methodologies, and a certain understanding of the behavior of elements studied. Teaching and learning futures studies for over a decade lends us important insights in this context.

Futures studies came into existence after the Second World War. American army-funded groups were involved in policy research, futures research. In 1967, the first conference was held in Oslo, Norway. The opinion among futures studies scholars on the "predicting" function is divided. The word future is a tantalizing one and predicting it with the "highest" precision is irresistible for all. A dominant school in futures studies considers it fit to predict a range of possible futures and posit desirable futures. Unfortunately, trouble-free and merry-go-round fortune telling is not the lot of futures studies. Futures studies is governed by principles of rigorous systems approach and objectivity. An amalgam of various techniques and synthesis of hard-earned wisdom of diverse disciplines are essential for it. It should have the competency to understand the prevailing paradigms and imminent shifts to present possible futures. By virtue of its uncertainty—for that matter, dealing with the future is always uncertain—it is only prudent to have greater interactions with other disciplines. Hence, there is a consensus that future prediction is not restricted necessarily to any isolated discipline and is interdisciplinary in nature.

Futures studies emphasizes an integrative holistic approach, as the task before it was once in the realm of the gods and the Delphic Oracle. And very much in the hands of shamans, priests, and medicine men too! What fate had befallen those diviners and their divinations, we may never come to know in full. But it serves as a reminder to tread cautiously, assimilate all that is related, persevere in gaining facts and findings, yet add a cautious footnote or two to the final output. Hence, the plethora of terms: possible futures, probable futures, alternate futures, and prescribing desirable futures. A strong interdisciplinary spirit is needed to govern the problem description, identify probable causes, guide forecasting, predict possible and desirable outcomes, and plan feasible actions to realize the planned future. All the while remembering that fantastic old Arabic saying: "Whoever predicts the future is a liar, even if what he tells is true."

This indeed is a formidable task. The ossified prejudices of many eminent and at once xenophobic scholars are not easily overcome. The regrettable speciation of disciplines is more the rule than the exception. However, the bedrock for the optimistic will to succeed and reconcile multiple disciplines towards a common goal is the continuous success of science throughout its history in overcoming the prevailing prejudices and misconceptions of the times. The acknowledgment of pioneering attempts has not always depended on the genius of the proponent who made the leap or the enormity of the output. It is rather the intellectual temper of the age that accords recognition. The intellectual temper can be very fickle or tolerant. The Church condemned Galileo for his heretical (but correct) beliefs and Darwin checked and rechecked his work on natural selection for two decades before daring to publish. Many a great philosopher was made a laughing stock in his time but they had the last laugh. The intellectual temper of contemporary society is worth reviewing here.

With the advent and spectacular growth of the World Wide Web and in what is termed a "Knowledge Era," the boundaries collapse in the same dramatic and significant way as did the Berlin Wall. They continue to collapse and the web acquires an increasingly stronger transdisciplinary hue. In its boundaryless environs, cross-pollination of ideas is facilitated and it is quite natural. With English emerging as the international medium of communication, there is no dearth of information. Recent phenomenal developments in technology have largely set us free from geographical boundaries.

This is further complemented by another major process currently in progress, namely globalization, which is in full swing, despite fierce resistance in some quarters. The debates on the benefits and perils of its progress will continue for a long time. Much in the same way debates have occurred in the course and in the aftermath of industrial revolution. But globalization is on us, and it is an indisputable fact. Business had already to a large extent taken on a transnational character. For the statistics, it is reported that the total number of transnational corporations in 1998 was 60,000 companies with 500,000 affiliates, compared with 37,000 transnational companies and 170,000 affiliates in 1990. Like a huge organism, the networked world conducts businesses spread over the planet. Interdisciplinary systems approach is the only way to comprehend whatever can be comprehended. This is because the pace of the whole process is not phased and gradual but, rather, cataclysmal. It breaches wall after wall of protectionist territories and like a tsunami overwhelms them. This necessitates a quick review of our establishments, education, culture, fitness, in short our perception of all that we do and hope to do.

To support the argument that isolation leads to dead-end evolution, we may draw a parallel from island biogeography, an absorbing transdisciplinary field. Charles Darwin and Alfred Wallace gained their famous insight on evolution through their studies in the Galapagos Islands and the Malay Archipelago respectively. Latter day island biogeographers established by studying islands and living beings that insular species eventually undergo morphological changes, such as gigantism or dwarfism, for instance, giant tortoises, Komodo dragons, pygmy elephants, and pygmy hippopotamuses. Both forms are extremes and hence more vulnerable to mass extinctions.

In the same way, insular disciplines tend to become more and more complex and thus acquire increasingly narrower bandwidths. They run the risk of eventually being so highly specialized that they are practically useless pursuits. Lack of applicability is the equivalent of biological extinction. Whenever the environment undergoes a drastic change, species have to adapt or face the fate of dinosaurs. Dinosaurs would never have considered it an incentive to get fossilized in order that some future Spielberg could gross his cool millions. Why should we yearn for fossilization? We have to adapt and be the fitter ones, for a simple reason called survival. The synergy from transdisciplinary skills facilitates growth and the aggregation of fitter disciplines ensures survival. Interestingly, information technology with its potential benefits has already achieved the genesis of new disciplines that are essentially interdisciplinary. Bioinformatics, geoinformatics and medical electronics are some such new additions.

A Review of Interdisciplinary Learning and Teaching in the Indian Context: Some Case Studies in Generating Development Solutions

The Centre for Futures Studies was founded in Madurai Kamaraj University in 1990. Eight such centers for future studies were established in Indian universities in that year but not many of them are still functional today. Apart from this department, none is functional in Tamil Nadu state and about three centers across the nation have done exceptionally well. In 1994, Madurai Kamaraj University senate upgraded the center into the Department of Futures Studies. Presently, it functions as a department under the School of Energy, Environment, and Natural Resources. The realignment is more in tune with current thinking which promotes interdisciplinarity among the departments. In many ways, Madurai Kamaraj University was a pioneer in introducing interdisciplinary learning in higher education. Even before futures studies was founded, it introduced biotechnology in 1985, almost immediately after the National Biotechnology Board (NBTB) introduced biotechnology as a focus area for support. Five universities began formal postgraduate courses in biotechnology in 1985 under the NBTB-University Grants Commission program of manpower development in the field. Today, 104 colleges offer biotechnology at the Bachelor of Engineering (B.E.) /Bachelor of Technology (B.Tech.) level. In Tamil Nadu alone, 36 colleges offer B.E. or B.Tech. in the subject.

In an interview for the Internet edition of *Frontline* magazine (*21*(13), June 19–July 2002) Mr Dharmalingam, Senior Professor and Head of the Department for Genetic Engineering in School of Biotechnology, cited the following pragmatic reason for not introducing the course at undergraduate level. "It is an interdisciplinary course where you need experts in chemistry, statistics, mathematics, microbiology, botany and zoology." He pointed out that it would be difficult to find experts to teach the subject at the undergraduate level as "biotechnology requires a level of knowledge at the master's level, not at the undergraduate level." Besides, it would be difficult to design a curriculum at the undergraduate level. He suggested that an "ideal" solution could lie in a dual-degree course that lasted four years. For instance, a student could do a B.Sc. in Microbiology for three years and do an advanced course in biotechnology in the fourth year.

In the same article, it is reported that the Mother Teresa Women's University, Kodaikanal, has already started experimenting with this double-degree program. Its Vice-Chancellor, Dr Anandhavalli Mahadevan, said the university would offer a "conceptual degree" at the end of three years of study and a vocational degree at the end of the fourth year. For instance, a student completing a B.A. in Geography could study tourism in the fourth year; a student completing a B.Sc. in Botany or Zoology could study biotechnology in the fourth year; and those who studied for a B.A. in English Literature could do visual communication or mass communication in the fourth year. It is heartening to learn of the spread of interdisciplinary approach in Tamil Nadu and university scenario in general.

The Futures Studies Department at Madurai Kamaraj University envisioned the following objectives at the start.

1. To introduce futures studies in higher education;
2. To promote research in futures studies;
3. To create awareness in futures studies through extension activities;
4. To foster the application of futures studies in user agencies like industries, planning cells, government, societies, employment organizations etc.

Year 2004 saw completion of the first decade for the department, and stocktaking is a useful way to document the key lessons learnt in imparting interdisciplinary learning in higher education, and of course the direction of progress. Initially the department offered a full-time Master of Philosophy (M.Phil.) program. Students with a postgraduate qualification were admitted. The program was designed to give training in forecasting techniques, holistic approach, systems approach, systems dynamics, data processing, and application in emerging and similar areas. Identifying emerging trends in fields like future materials, energy, technology, education, and environmental risk assessment were stressed. Far from being restricted to classroom sessions, fieldwork and projects with social relevance were part of the curriculum. Simultaneously Ph.D. programs were offered. A number of meaningful projects with an interdisciplinary approach were conceived; and a representative list of Ph.D. works in critical areas is given below. While Ph.D. as well as M.Phil. studies are in various fields, the general undercurrent governing the studies is planning and assisting planning. There are forecasting projects as well. The established futures studies techniques have been applied in the following areas:

Education
- Science curriculum in school education;
- Futuristic study of environmental education.

Environment
- Developing environmental design and evolving perspective land use planning for Pondicherry union territory;
- Assessing ecological imbalance of the Palani hills and conservation of the shola forests using GIS and remote sensing technologies;

- Planning and management of the Therkar watershed through GIS and remote sensing technologies.

Urban management
- Composite landscape assessment of Madurai Metropolitan Region—a GIS approach;
- A systems dynamics simulation model for development of Madurai district.

Rural industry
- A study of production-planning and inventory control in small-scale industries.

Society
- A study of the role of judiciary in Indian political system—a futuristic approach.

The Master of Philosophy projects were even more varied in their subject matter:

Agriculture
- Indian cardamom and its futures;
- Rubber production and its futures;
- Rainwater harvesting for future domestic water supply to Ramanathapuram city.

Rural industry
- Assessment of occupational hazards of various industries in Sivakasi Taluk;
- Trends in production of cotton cloth in Tamil Nadu by 2007;
- A futuristic assessment of animal husbandry programs in T. Kalupatti.

Energy
- Wind power generation at Kayathar—a futuristic study;
- Integrated rural energy systems for district livestock farm at Nellai—a computer simulation model.

While these were some of the projects completed, the curriculum design that enabled the work is elaborated below.

M. Phil. programs were run for two semesters and a project was to be completed by the students. The broad categories taught and constituent elements are briefly illustrated.

Paper I: Introduction to Futures Studies and Research

1. Basic concepts—ten hours
   Need for Futures research—Views about Futures—Characteristics of Futures—Extrapolative Futures—Normative Futures—Preparing for

the Futures—Concept of change—Need for planning—Strategic perspective planning—Short range planning—Goal setting—Generating alternatives—Decision making-SWOT-AHP

2. Concepts—twenty hours
Systems analysis and modeling—Systems approach—Systems structure—Systems behavior—Systems state—Types of systems, entities, attributes and measurement—System dynamics—Types of models—Verification and validation of models

3. Technology Forecasting—seven hours
Technology—Stages of technology innovation—Rapid changes in technological scene—Need for technology forecasting and its use

4. Technology Assessment—ten hours
Basic aspects—Types of assessment—Introduction to technology assessment and environmental impact assessment—Components of technology assessment—Definitions, boundaries—Technology descriptions—Technology forecasting—Social forecasting—Impact identification, analysis and evaluation—Policy analysis and communication

5. Social forecasting—seven hours
Needs—Social indicators—Social forecasting

6. Research Methodology and Design—six hours
Hypothesis—Research design—Sampling techniques—Project proposals and presentation.

Paper II: Forecasting Techniques—Introduction to Forecasting Techniques and Classification

1. Short and medium range forecasting—fifteen hours
Time series models—Moving averages—Box Jenkins—Smoothing techniques—Arima models

2. Long-range forecasting—five hours
Introduction—Issues in long range forecasting.

3. Exploratory methods—ten hours
Trend extrapolation and substitution techniques—Growth curves—Simulation techniques—Brainstorming—Delphi-Cross Impact analysis—Scenario building—Elementary systems dynamics

4. Normative Methods—twenty hours
Surveys—Expert panels—Scenarios—Relevance trees—Morphological analysis—Overview of operation research models

5. Merits and limitations of forecasting methods—ten hours
Breakthroughs and innovations—Limitations of different forecasting methods—Errors in technological forecasting—Combining forecast.

Paper III: Environmental Impact Assessment

Introduction and need for EIA—Features and components of technology assessment and EIA—Aspects of bounding and analytical strategies—Impact classification—Methodologies for impact assessment—Ecological impact—Socio-economic impact—Practical consideration for EIA—Risk assessment and hazard management—Valuation of non-market goods.

Paper IV: Project Work in Any of the Above Areas

Ph.D. scholars are guided in their methodology selection and are trained in hypothesis formation, statistical techniques and necessary research methods. The scholar is expected to satisfactorily demonstrate suitability of the methodology in the methodology review. Usually, a doctoral research is completed in about four years.

In teaching and guiding the students to adopt an interdisciplinary approach to complete the projects, the curriculum design is found to be generally adequate. There is stress on an eclectic choice of suitable techniques to address the core issues. The increasing choice of Geographic Information Systems to develop solutions for landscape assessment, watershed management, and ecological issues appears to be an outcome of the strong emphasis on interdisciplinary approach. Also, the social bent/orientation in the project selection is in line with the objectives of the department.

However, the enrolment of students in the M.Phil. program was not up to expectations. In all, the department has awarded the degree to 55 students since inception of the course in 1991. After reviewing the drop in enrolment and organizational constraints, the department evolved a strategy of offering the constituent parts of the course to postgraduate students as elective subjects in what is called a Choice-Based Credit System (CBCS). After an initial lukewarm response, the strategy worked and greater numbers of students evinced a keen interest in pursuing the course. From five students in the year 2000 the enrolment went up to a healthy 35 in 2002, then 42, and 45 in successive years. The students are from diverse disciplines like biology, sociology, geography, environmental remote sensing and cartography, English, journalism, and chemistry.

The Choice-Based Credit System offers the ten elective courses. Each elective course carries four credits. The scheme of examinations is divided into internal assessment (40 percentage marks) and external assessment (60 percentage marks) and the pass minimum is 50 percentage marks. The electives are listed below:

- Introduction to Futures Studies
- Using Systems approaches
- Futures workshop
- Urban Futures

- Science, Technology, Society and Futures
- Decision-making models for the Futures
- Business Forecasting
- Environmental Impact Assessment
- Sustainable and Global Futures
- Women's Futures

Of the ten courses offered, the most popular choices are Using Systems approaches, Environmental Impact Assessment, Urban Futures, Women's Futures and Science, Technology, Society and Futures. The choices of students are influenced by the relative accessibility of the elective in terms of its relationship with their chosen disciplines. For instance, the Environmental Remote Sensing students chose Environmental Impact Assessment and Sociology students chose Women's Futures or Science, Technology, Society Futures as their elective. But the students were seen to express satisfaction on the course content.

The Tenth Plan guidelines issued by University Grants Commission invited

> proposals for specialized courses at undergraduate and post graduate levels including postgraduate diplomas in Interdisciplinary and Emerging Areas and accommodate brilliant ideas and innovative proposals to influence teaching, research, academic excellence, societal growth and relevant activities in various disciplines which meet educational, national and global priorities.

The Department of Futures Studies, consolidating the experience gained through varied programs offered so far, has proposed a postgraduate course, Master of Science in Futures Studies. The rationale is that the introduction of an interdisciplinary course at undergraduate level is unlikely to offer the necessary focus for the students. A postgraduate course with application orientation is the right level at which to take forward the teaching of interdisciplinarity. The proposal is under consideration.

On redesigning the syllabus, a growing constancy of analytical tools and theoretical elements could be discerned. Trend analysis extrapolation, cross-impact analysis, systems approach, Delphi, relevance tree and morphological analysis, analytical hierarchy process, and other such established techniques have remained unchanged as part of the curriculum over the years. Meanwhile the philosophical views on futures studies are witnessing radical changes. Richard Slaughter put forth his recommendations for a knowledge-base model featuring internal and external synthesis and layering of core elements in 1993. The interpretations found in the discussions of contemporary futurists like Sohail Inayatullah, James Dator, Zia Sardar (to name just a few) and the influence of postmodernist philosophy are too profound to be ignored. For instance, the pregnant question of James Dator "If Futures Studies can know nothing about the Future, what use is it?" is noteworthy. Equally valid are the social considerations of Wendell, Hazel Henderson, and Massini. On one hand the decade-long experience in teaching futures Studies points to an emerging disciplinarity. On the other hand the need to regularly review and incorporate the theoretical aspects of the field into the curriculum is also keenly felt.

In the Indian context, the lack of acknowledgement of new studies in terms of employment opportunities is a significant deterrent to the spread and success of interdisciplinary teaching. No academic institution can forego its responsibility of enabling the students to survive in the market place. Although the courses cover a lot of analytical techniques in greater depth than a management course does, there are no convincing employment opportunities for those who have completed a futures studies course. This dampens the spirit of the students to opt for new interdisciplinary courses. The successful spread of biotechnology coincides with the increased absorption of students into the flourishing biotechnology industry.

From this standpoint, if as common a syllabus as possible across the world for postgraduate students of futures studies could be evolved, an increased acknowledgement for the course can be anticipated. Inter-university dialogues on the upgrading of teaching and learning will also augment the quality of the courses. It is pertinent to note that the University Grants Commission and other policy-making bodies have spelt out their preference for an interdisciplinary approach to meet national and global needs.

The confidence and inspiration of proposing a full-time course in futures studies was the experiences gained in two key projects undertaken in 1996 and 1999. The World Futures Studies Federation initiated a global visions project and students from 15 different countries were engaged in this futures-visioning project. This department took it to students of different disciplines in many colleges affiliated to the university and several departments within it. After familiarizing the selected participants with each other, training in futures visioning was given and the visions were consolidated. The visioning process was an object lesson on the fruitfulness of interdisciplinary interactions.

In the Millennium project, the department acted as a nodal agency in India and over 300 participants contributed to the identification of challenges ahead, with a focus on visions of the future and improvements in the decision process that can help close the gap between early future-oriented alerts and timely action. Related issues such as ethics and environmental security were also explored. The interaction with diverse disciplines world over greatly contributed to the understanding of key methodologies and the identification of impediments and possible alternatives.

For Indian policy makers it is an acknowledged priority to increase the use of technology to address key development issues such as rural development, water resource management, amelioration of environmental degradation, urban town planning, etc. The information required for framing the development policies are drawn from varied sources and quite often, the data retrieval is found to be an involved process, time-consuming, susceptible to error, and sometimes obsolete. The lack of a proper information system to support decision-making was keenly felt. Given the size, complexities, and geographic variations within the country, any attempt to invest in building a nationwide information system all at once will prove to be costly and may even turn out to be counterproductive. A further aspect that compounded the issue was the number of departments involved in data collection for the government and, importantly, the quality of the spatial data, since they do not reflect the landscape changes and are out of date. The Indian Space Research Organization had spent staggering amounts to launch satellites, a Herculean task in this impoverished country and a sin if not put to best use. The remote sensing data acquired can readily be used to update the maps, provided an interdisciplinary approach is employed. The need for building prototype models to demonstrate viability, usefulness, and scope for refinement was expressed. The academic community was invited to offer suitable technology solutions.

True to its objectives, the Department of Futures Studies formulated such models and proposed them to various government development agencies. Geographic Information System (GIS) was identified as the possible solution. The disciplines that constituted the solution were, geography, geology, remote sensing, cartography, Global Positioning Systems (GPS), with information technology elements and Geographic Information Systems (GIS) software integrating all.

Case Study

Decision Support System for Policy Planners and Executors
Rural Area Development Monitoring and Information System (RAMIS)

This prototype is aimed at assisting decision makers like district collectors as well as the rural public by providing faster access to integrated information. About 1,800 hardcopy maps covering 5,000 square kilometers have to be scanned and digitized. There are 50 spatial data points, e.g., location of round well, square well, bore well, culvert, bridge, foot path, cart track, etc. to be linked with 400 attributes in a seamless map of the total area. All these details are essential to prioritize development funding and monitoring progress. Data from the Indian Remote Sensing Satellite P6 with 5.8-meter multi-spectral resolution are to be digitally processed and superimposed over the survey maps to make them contemporary. Specific locations will be georeferenced through Global Positioning System (GPS). By georeferencing, available data are updated. In order to disseminate information to all sections of the society, there are attempts to provide the entire information in vernacular Tamil and English. This will enable the stakeholders to undertake active participation in development plans and claim priorities.

This project integrates the fruits of various disciplines and presents it in such a way that technology is put to best use by the development authorities as well as the rural masses. Incidentally, this is the first time GPS is being used at the largest scale and maps are available in the state combined as a mosaic.

Similar projects for landscape assessment, water resource management, town planning, and management have been undertaken to demonstrate the practical competence of the core group of the department.

Summary

The lessons learnt from the case studies and things that went wrong and that are still going wrong are numerous. But the overwhelming satisfaction derived from the work is the realization that an interdisciplinary study is a meaningful synthesis of the best practices in the constituent disciplines to address the problems. Using high-end computers, prohibitively costly software, complex remote sensing data, GPS supported by several satellites, all to bring a change in the life of a peasant with meager land holdings, is a wonderful feeling. The fulfillment of social responsibility will continue to be one of the key motivators even in the globalization epoch.

This is of course one side of it. The other side is also relevant. The hardships in the field in the collection of data, the laborious digitization process, project time overruns, delays in funding, unforgivable bugs in programs cropping up in the middle of presentations are all valuable, at least when seen in retrospect. These difficulties remind us of the enormity of the task ahead and the need to fine tune. The policy executives now evince more interest in interdisciplinary approaches in the search for development solutions. A thousand power point presentations on the potential benefits of an integrated approach could have achieved only more smothered yawns. That there is something tangible to look at which explores possible uses has opened a floodgate of interest. The learning and teaching of the interdisciplinary approach to address the management of development issues has not been in vain. More than the mechanical turning out of more and more students, the experiences gained in the practical projects make us realize the need to change with the times and the importance of an integrated approach.

Further Reading

Bell, W. (1997). *Foundations of Futures Studies*. New Brunswick: Transaction Publishers.

Bonner, J. T. (1970). *The Scale of Nature*. Tadworth, Surrey: Worlds Work Limited.

Buzan, B., and Segal, G. (1998). *Anticipating the future: Twenty millennia of human progress*. London: Simon and Schuster.

Mazzarr, M. J. (1999). *Global trends 2005. An owner's manual for the next decade*. New York: St Martin's Press.

Quammen, D. (1998). *The song of the dodo: Island biogeography in the age of extinctions* (Indian reprint). New Delhi: David Frank Bros & Co.

14
Interdisciplinarity in Learning and Teaching in Religious Studies

MELANIE J. WRIGHT AND JUSTIN MEGGITT

University of Cambridge

Background

Practitioners of religious studies have long understood their field to be an interdisciplinary one. Indeed, the institutionalization of religious studies within higher education was itself partly aided by changes in the structure and culture of British universities from the 1960s onwards, which allowed for flexibility and cooperation between previously boundaried departments. Whereas academic theology originated in the training of Christian clergy in medieval Europe, religious studies has its roots in three traditions. The first two are the Orientalists' fascination with "the East," and *Religionswissenschaft*—the "scientific" study of religion as articulated in the nascent human sciences (anthropology, psychology, sociology). The third is the practice of comparative religion, by which students aimed to understand particular traditions, usually in relation to categories derived from their own dominant domestic tradition (typically, Western Christianity); in this they were motivated at least partly by a desire to demonstrate either its shortcomings or its strengths (Cox, 1998, pp. 1–2; Sharpe, 1986, p. 2; Theology and Religious Studies Benchmarking Group, 2000, p. 2).

Contemporary religious studies is distinguished from these endeavors by an attitude that is non-confessional without discounting religiosity, but its polygenesis is reflected in an ongoing preoccupation with method and theory (an impulse recently strengthened by the impact of postmodernism, postcolonialism, and the related problems of epistemology). Small wonder that in addressing the British Association for the Study of Religions (BASR) in 2000, Brian Bocking observed, "to think of the Study of Religions . . . as a 'discipline' hardly fits the case" (2004, p. 11).

Arguably, then, satisfactory work in this field presumes (at least) openness to the possibility of interdisciplinarity. Indeed, there are impulses evident within the current practice of religious studies in Britain that seem to encourage the active adoption of interdisciplinarity. On the one hand, a multifactorial approach is taken that can be located in the traditional search for a wide-ranging, total knowledge of one's subject. On the other, it can be seen as born of a desire to question our attempts to organize and communicate knowledge, and to address issues that are marginal to traditional ways of approaching a discipline (Moran, 2002, 15). Whilst one might find both kinds of impulses behind teaching and learning in religious studies at both undergraduate and postgraduate level, arguably, one most readily finds the quest for total knowledge at the undergraduate level, whereas at Master's level and beyond, students may be more frequently engaged in the business of interdisciplinary work in the more radical sense of subverting or doing away with traditional categories of knowledge.

Pragmatic factors also encourage interdisciplinarity (or the rhetoric of interdisciplinarity) in religious studies. Policy initiatives and market forces foster a de-emphasis on older configurations of knowledge as governments and employers ask teachers to evaluate academic competence in relation to transferable skills and competencies (the shift from "what do students understand?" to "what can they do?").

Shifts in the teaching of religious studies in secondary schools also lay the foundations for interdisciplinarity or transdisciplinarity at degree level. The new specifications for AS-level Religious Studies require students to focus on one or more religions across a range of areas including ethics, history, philosophy, psychology, sociology, and textual studies. A-level candidates must complete a synoptic assessment, drawing together knowledge, understanding, and skills learned across the course (Hayward, 2000, sections 2.1 and 2.3). Given that the increasing numbers of A-level candidates (in 2004 religious studies saw the largest percentage increase in candidates of any subject, a rise of 13.8 percent) constitute an important pool of potential religious studies undergraduates, recruitment and teaching in higher education are being inexorably affected by such developments. Finance requires that many institutions now offer religion courses, like other "minority" subjects, exclusively or primarily within combined honors programs. But the most common site of interdisciplinarity in Britain today—and the one least recognized as such, by teachers and learners alike—remains the "Theology and Religious Studies" (TRS) degree, a program which attempts to hold in balance (or tension) confessional and non-confessional positions. In some cases this offering results from student demand or faculty anticipation (for example, the desire to enhance a theology department's traditional focus on topics of Christian interest). In others, it is a function as much of budget management and administration as it is of the older discipline's recognition and acceptance of newer fields and forms of knowledge. Accordingly, in contemporary Britain a good deal of interdisciplinarity in religious studies learning and teaching is as accidental (therefore unthinking, vulnerable to retrenchment) as it is ubiquitous.

Indeed, several factors militate against the successful development and sustainability of a culture of interdisciplinarity within religious studies. If intellectual and institutional concerns may on occasion foster a drive to inter-disciplinarity, the work of funding and evaluation bodies exerts a powerful draw-back to longer established disciplinary labels and cultures. As its name suggests, the Quality Assurance Agency (QAA) for Higher Education's process of "subject review" fosters a view of isolated departments or "compartments" (Bocking, 2004, p. 12) of learning (on this see more later, "Case Study"). Similarly, the QAA Benchmarking Statement for religious studies links it with theology, privileging one kind of interdisciplinary contact (and with it, the activities which the two disciplines hold in common, such as textual study) whilst implicitly demoting or downplaying others (Theology and Religious Studies Benchmarking Group, 2000). As in other areas, the full significance of the benchmarking statement remains to be seen, but what is clear is that it is an increasingly important point of reference not just for external review bodies but also internally for institutions as they design and evaluate new programs.

Likewise the Research Assessment Exercise (RAE) appears to function as an inhibitor of interdisciplinarity in religious studies. Since its inception, the RAE's critics have complained that the requirement for research activity to be associated with a discipline-based "Unit of Assessment" limits the scope for interdisciplinarity. Although official reports to date have suggested that there is no evidence that the RAE systematically discriminates against interdisciplinary research, it remains that there is a significant impression that it does so. Given that perceptions about the RAE dominate the practices and decision-making that shape much of contemporary academic life (and consequently teaching and learning in religious studies) this belief is significant. Tellingly, the sum-mary statement of the latest RAE panel in religious studies lamented the lack of high-quality interdisciplinary work within the field. Whatever its stated intentions, so far the RAE's mechanisms evidently have not encouraged interdisciplinarity.

Within religious studies, more widely perceived problems in relation to funding, evaluation, and interdisciplinarity are perhaps particularly acute. Those who make decisions about opportunities and resourcing within the field—which, crucially, for RAE as for QAA purposes, is grouped with theology—tend in many cases not to be religious studies practitioners them-selves, but are instead (in a reflection of the traditional balance of power between the different groups engaged in the academic study of the phenom-enon of religion in the U.K.) theologians drawn from institutions that operate a conservative understanding of the field and its potential for interaction with other disciplines. As Alastair Hunter (2005, p. 24) observes, a recent mono-graph by members of the Theology and Religious Studies section of the British Academy (Nicholson [Ed.], 2004) conceives of the field in strikingly narrow terms. Amongst other things, it neglects to discuss the study of Hinduism, Islam, modern Judaism, or Buddhism in Britain, and theoretical models ubi-quitous in religious studies (where they are strongly associated with the kind of synoptic interdiscipinarity discussed earlier) such as that of Ninian Smart are also absent. Even within the discussions of the traditional specialisms represented by the contributors themselves, attempts at interdisciplinarity are given little attention: for example, within the sub-field of biblical studies, the impact of literary theory and feminist criticism seem to have largely passed the contributors by.

Finally, away from the realm of governmental initiatives, the impact of private funding on the establishment and maintenance of posts and resources may also militate against the development of interdisciplinarity. Religious studies in the U.K. has (relative to other arts subjects) attracted considerable support from non-governmental sources, particularly individual benefactors. However, for the most part, private donors are concerned with promoting or ensuring the confessional study of their own particular religious tradition. This cuts across the traditionally non-confessional ethos of religious studies. Moreover, the concerns and consequences of interdisciplinarity are rarely congruent with such agendas. As the U.K. higher education sector becomes increasingly privatized, the role of donors will become more significant and the educational culture created may well be one less conducive to interdisciplinarity. Of course, such developments are not necessarily negative. The John Templeton Foundation, for example, although having its own ideological concerns, is a major funder of research and teaching on the interfaces between religion and science; the research, teaching, and learning it seeks to initiate and foster is avowedly interdisciplinary. Nevertheless, in most instances non-governmental funding seems more likely to be an inhibitor of than a stimulus for interdisciplinarity in religious studies.

Having briefly reviewed the contested origins and prospects of interdisciplinarity within religious studies, we will now turn briefly to a current example of interdisciplinarity in practice.

Case Study

This case study concerns the development of an interdisciplinary Master's degree in Jewish-Christian Relations, taught by the Centre for the Study of Jewish-Christian Relations in Cambridge (and by distance learning) and validated by Anglia Polytechnic University (APU). Since initial planning in 1998, the M.A. has been conceived as interdisciplinary. To date, around 70 students have graduated from the program; collectively, their dissertations bring together insights from religious studies with those of art history, biblical studies, education studies, history, linguistics, literature, philosophy, politics, psychoanalysis, theology, and women's studies. Perhaps inevitably for such a project, however, the M.A. continues to exist in a kind of dynamic tension as teachers and learners alike negotiate a number of disciplinary pulls. These are apparent on examination of teaching and learning on the course. They also operate at structural/managerial levels, since whilst the M.A. course ethos evokes that of non-confessional religious studies, for administrative purposes it is homed within a "Theology" set at APU, and its sister programs within this set are all designed to form part of the training of Christian ministers, and require a faith commitment on the part of students. We have already suggested that this type of arrangement is itself not untypical, insofar as there is an established history of such forms of multi- or interdisciplinary "cooperation" between the various disciplines that engage in the academic study of religions in Britain.

A number of reasons lay behind the MA's interdisciplinary approach, as it was first delineated:

1. The development of the field

Jewish-Christian relations was a comparatively new field of study in the 1990s (and remains so today). In addressing many topics in the relations between Jews and Christians (and Judaism and Christianity) teachers and learners would be breaking new ground. A multifactoral, interdisciplinary approach would militate against the potential for artificial or reductionist constructions of realities.

2. Precedent in cognate fields

The related (but distinct) field of holocaust studies, in which people use tools and insights from a range of disciplines (either discretely or in combination) in order to tackle broadly related questions, provided a useful precedent for an interdisciplinary approach to Jewish-Christian relations.

3. Recruitment

It was envisaged that the M.A. would attract some recent graduates, but that most potential students would be more mature learners, with diverse (sometimes diffuse) expectations and needs, not readily confined by the approach of a single discipline. An interdisciplinary program would cater for these interests.

In order to meet these aims, the course structure required students to take one compulsory or "core" module before choosing a further three modules from a list of options, covering different aspects of Jewish-Christian relations. Initially, the optional modules were fairly "disciplinary" in character (e.g. a historical module on nineteenth-century European Jewish-Christian relations; a module on Jewish-Christian relations, literature, and film), with significant emphasis being placed on the core module as integrative—with the final dissertation, the most obvious locus of interdisciplinary work on the M.A.

It soon became apparent, however, that this arrangement was not as successful as initially hoped. The siting of the course within the theology set entailed involvement in forms of subject review and evaluation (both internal and external) that sent strong messages to students and staff about "center" and "periphery" within the program. Student feedback suggested that whilst many arrived expecting an interdisciplinary religious studies program, they implicitly learnt that the study of visual media (for example) or literary texts, were the hors-d'oeuvre before the more serious work of scriptural or historical analysis. Teachers similarly reported concerns as students tended to use methods and concepts from other disciplines as if they were uncontested. This happened particularly at the dissertation stage, where the work of weaker students was non-disciplinary, in the sense of being uncritical, assuming too many givens and so on.

Revealingly, when it came to editing the text of the Self-Assessment Document, prior to the QAA Subject Review of Theology and Religious Studies at the University of Cambridge in 2001, we found ourselves switching "multidisciplinary" for "interdisciplinary" at numerous points in the text, in recognition of the fact that we were only partly there.

Measures were initiated to rectify this. For example, we designed a further group of study skills seminars running alongside the modules, and taking place throughout the academic year, with the intention that interdisciplinarity remained a regular and recurrent academic concern of the participants. Greater emphasis was placed on the requirement of a detailed proposal for work at the dissertation stage, when students' interdisciplinary practice is typically more overt. This functioned to push students to design research and become more conscious of the instrumental value of interdisciplinarity in successfully scrutinizing their chosen research question. Interestingly, this type of practical approach to interdisciplinary work contrasts with the requirement in schools for pupils to demonstrate synoptic work for A-level assessment that we have noted above. We also rethought the content of the component modules so that regardless of the particular configuration of options chosen by the students, there was a clear integration between their initial introduction to interdisciplinarity in the foundation module and their subsequent encounters with its practice. On reflection it was evident that we had assumed that the foundation module could inculcate the practice of interdisciplinarity in isolation from the other modules. For learning on the whole of the the the course to be demonstrably interdisciplinary, rather than multidisciplinary, interdisciplinarity must be experienced and employed as an overt, repeated, and in some sense, familiar, undertaking, throughout the program.

On further critical reflection, one unexpected feature of the M.A.'s development has encouraged us to consider the actual (as opposed to the intended) nature of interdisciplinarity as experienced by students: the program has attracted a surprisingly high proportion of non-U.K. students. To date around a quarter of all students (and a majority of those who have studied the degree full time in Cambridge) have been "international," representing a range of countries including Argentina, Australia, Canada, Czech Republic, Hungary, Irish Republic, Israel, Japan, Macedonia, New Zealand, Poland, Russia, and the U.S. This has impacted teaching and learning across the M.A., particularly in relation to interdisciplinarity and the related issue of critical thinking (on the latter see Bennett Moore et al., 2003, especially pp. 86–88). The presence of international learners can provide a valuable opportunity to consider the cultural constructedness and specificity of teaching, learning, and assessment in the study of religion. Indeed, the differing approaches and competencies advocated by an internationally diverse group of students (who may all hold similarly named qualifications in religious studies!) introduces a kind of de facto interdisciplinarity into the classroom, which good teachers may use to good effect at Master's level. At the same time, it is evident that the practice of interdisciplinarity is additionally problematized for learners who start from a context where their "home" discipline, and even the notion of disciplinarity itself, is defined differently than it is in the U.K. For example, whilst U.K. students with a background in religious studies need to develop a familiarity with the methods of literary and/or cinema studies in order to negotiate successfully the optional module, "Jews and Christians, Literature and Film," international learners may have added to this the burden of learning new ways of defining and doing religious studies. All this may constitute not just an intellectual problem, but also a personal/emotional hurdle for international learners, for whom a specific type of disciplinary proficiency ("the way we do things at home") is an important part of their identity whilst living and studying abroad. (Jan Parker's [2002] notion of the discipline as a community, culture, or territory, which one "inhabits" and seeks to defend in the face of perceived attack, is relevant here.)

The Interdisciplinarity Future

The future of interdisciplinarity in teaching and learning in religious studies is a problematic one. There are, as we noted at the outset, significant factors, intrinsic to the history and practice of the discipline itself, as well as some that are pragmatic in nature, that would seem to encourage the increased deployment and development of interdisciplinarity. If this is the case then there will be fascinating and exciting consequences: what constitutes "religious studies" will itself be transformed by such work. Indeed, despite its limitations and challenges, this has been our experience of learning and teaching undertaken in the M.A. in Jewish-Christian Relations. Courses such as ours, which seek to implement the overt practice of interdisciplinarity, help to ensure that religious studies is not left as students first encountered it.

However, we cannot assume that the practice of interdisciplinarity will be significant in the future of religious studies, whatever its apparent benefits. The (largely) governmental and institutional factors that are impeding its development may continue to stifle innovation. Nonetheless we should end this piece on an optimistic note. Philip Esler, a notable practitioner and advocate for interdisciplinarity within the field (as broadly construed—see, for example Esler, 1994 and Esler and Boyd, 2004), has recently been appointed the Chief Executive of the AHRC, the primary public funding body for research and postgraduate study within the arts and humanities in the U.K. Although it will take more than one appointment to overcome governmental obstacles to the practice of interdisciplinarity in religious studies, it is a hopeful indication that the future may be rather more positive than it might otherwise appear.

References

Bennett Moore, Z., Faltin, L., and Wright, M. J. (2003). Critical thinking and international post-graduate students' discourse. *Learning and Teaching in Philosophical and Religious Studies, 3*(1), 63–94.

Bocking, B. (2004). *The study of religions: The new queen of the sciences?* Occasional Paper 21, Leeds: British Association for the Study of Religions.

Cox, J. L. (1998). *Alterity as identity: Innovation in the academic study of religions.* Occasional Paper 18, Leeds: British Association for the Study of Religions.

Esler, P. (1994). *First Christians in their social worlds: Social-scientific approaches to New Testament interpretation.* London: Routledge.

Esler, P., and Boyd, J. (2004). *Visuality and biblical text: Interpreting Velázquez' Christ with Martha and Mary as a test case.* Florence: Leo S. Olschki Editore.

Hayward, M. (2000). *Recognising the changing face of religious studies at GCE AS and A Level* [online]. Leeds: The Higher Education Academy Philosophical and Religious Studies Subject Centre. Retrieved June 1, 2005 from http://www.prs.heacademy.ac.uk/relig_studies/articles/hayward1/index.html.

Hunter, A. (2005). Perspective distorted by cloistered views. *Times Higher Education Supplement* January 14, 24.

Moran, J. (2002). *Interdisciplinarity.* London: Routledge.

Nicholson, E. (Ed.) (2004). *A century of theological and religious studies in Britain, 1902–2002.* Oxford: Oxford University Press.

Parker, J. (2002). *Teaching in Higher Education, 7*(4), 373–386.

Sharpe, E. (1986). *Comparative religion: A history.* London: Duckworth.

Theology and Religious Studies Benchmarking Group (2000). *Theology and religious studies. Subject Benchmarking Statement.* Gloucester: Quality Assurance Agency for Higher Education.

Conclusion
Towards Interdisciplinarity in the Twenty-First Century

BALASUBRAMANYAM CHANDRAMOHAN

Kingston University

AND

STEPHEN FALLOWS

University of Chester

Trends Past and Present

Interdisciplinary study is rapidly becoming the norm for many students—traditional "disciplines" are losing their appeal and are being replaced by new theme-based programs.

Interdisciplinary themes evolve, not always linearly, into larger units, such as subjects, fields, etc., shaped by taxonomies of knowledge, blue skies and applied research, organizational structures, and communities of practice that encompass interactions beyond a specific discipline. Interdisciplinarity, thus, leads to the development of new disciplines.

The new disciplines are often more career-focussed than were previous ones. Vocational relevance is a major driving force in the development of multi/transdisciplinary programs/teams.

What Are the Implications?

Higher education institutions face new tensions as student numbers and teaching-based funding shift away from departments focussed on "old" disciplines. The new units/departments stand to benefit from the situation. For example, in the sciences traditional physics, biology, and chemistry departments are "dying," but new areas such as forensic science and nanotechnology are emerging. Humanistic disciplines such as philosophy, literature, and art are losing out to media studies, tourism or business studies.

These tensions create new divisions in academia, leading to a pecking order based on assumptions of academic rigor in specific programs or disciplines. Disciplines seen as "soft" become metaphors for the "dumbing down" of higher education, as in the case of media studies being seen as a "Micky Mouse" subject. Some academic establishments do not even recognize pre-university qualifications in such subjects.

The newness that the interdisciplinary crossing of boundaries generates in learning and teaching is an opportunity or a threat depending on the institution and how it sees itself as a gatekeeper of quality and standards. Long-established disciplines benefit from the assumptions of the solidity of scholarship in their area, while the new and, often, vocational areas experience a skeptical reception. In such situations interdisciplinary endeavor could extend the boundaries of "old" disciplines rather than lead to the establishment of a new disciplines.

The Challenge

Academic disciplines rise and fall depending on the demand for specific skills in a time/space framework. While individuals in pursuit of knowledge in earlier periods did not recognize strict divisions in terms of branches of knowledge or even professions—the Renaissance ideal saw little difference between a poet and a man of science—the institutionalized pursuit of knowledge responded more closely to the demands of the economy and social engineering. The need for specialization for industrial efficiency in nineteenth-century Europe and North America saw the emergence of teaching institutions and consolidation of a specific taxonomy of knowledge that survived much of the twentieth century. Similarly, the emergence of English as a "teachable" area of knowledge owes its usefulness to the social and colonial situation of the eighteenth century.

However, it is not all *déjàvu*. The rapid expansion of communication technologies and access to information has made the crossing of boundaries between disciplines a global phenomenon. The evolution of disciplines and the emergence of interdisciplines, with the reworking of definitions and structures that this implies, is likely to involve intellectual traditions, communities of practice and validation from across the globe in a much more overt way than in the age of industrialization.

Interdisciplinarity in teaching and learning in higher education involves a range of institutional adjustments that are not easily accommodated within the subject-bound ethos of most institutions. The challenge of interdisciplinarity for learning and teaching lies, often, in overcoming the mismatch between the level of interest in starting multi/interdisciplinary courses and preparedness to undertake changes in organizational structures. Several institutions are motivated by the marketability of multi/interdisciplinary courses, but are slow to provide supporting structures to deliver interdisciplinary courses effectively.

Developing and strengthening institutional infrastructure in the horizontal areas is as important as promoting the vertical aspects, as the different chapters in the book highlight.

Index